Who's Who in Britain's Bloody Crown

A Tudor Times Insight

By Tudor Times

Published by Tudor Times Ltd

## Tudor Times Insights

Tudor Times Insights are books collating articles from our website www.tudortimes.co.uk which is a repository for a wide variety of information about the Tudor and Stewart period 1485 – 1625. There you can find material on People, Places, Daily Life, Military & Warfare, Politics & Economics and Religion. The site has a Book Review section, with author interviews and a book club. It also features comprehensive family trees, and a 'What's On' event list with information about forthcoming activities relevant to the Tudors and Stewarts.

**Titles in the Series**

*Profiles*

*People*

*Politics & Economy*

# Contents

## Preface

The period of the Wars of the Roses was one of the most bloody in English history. The rival royal families of Lancaster and York and their noble followers fought for over thirty years for dominance of crown and country. The history is brilliantly retold in Dan Jones' 'The Hollow Crown' published by Faber & Faber in April 2015. (The US title is The Wars of the Roses)

The book was adapted by UK's Channel 5 in a mini-series that has been widely enjoyed. However, the huge numbers of protagonists involved, the similarity of names across generation and the frequency with which the nobles changed sides, often motivated by revenge or profit, make identifying everyone difficult.

This book lists all of the individuals mentioned by Jones in his book, and gives summary facts about them, for easy reference to the book, the series, or any other material on the Wars of the Roses.

What is terrifying is the sheer quantity of individuals killed in battle or immediately after, executed, assassinated or lynched!

The material was first published on www.tudortimes.co.uk

## A Guide to the Personalities in Channel 5's Britain's Bloody Crown

The entries give some key facts about the individuals who played a part, whether large or small, in the period known as the Wars of the Roses. The Channel 5 series is based on the excellent 'The Hollow Crown', by Dan Jones, who also presents the television programme. Jones mentions an enormous range of individuals, many of whom have the same names and titles. The list below summarises the key facts about each one. Although some of the protagonists always supported either Lancaster or York, many changed allegiance over the period, so it is not possible to give a definitive attribution to either party.

### Ordering of Entries

Monarchs and other people with no known surname are listed alphabetically under their first names.

Women are listed under the name used by Jones, with their maiden names in brackets.

 Denotes killed in battle. There is a list of the battles and dates at the end.

 Denotes executed, whether by due process; summary execution after a battle; or lynching.

All dates are new style, with the year beginning on 1 January.

**Andre to Dudley**

# A

**Andre, Bernard, circa 1450 – 1522** Andre was a French Augustinian friar appointed by Henry VII to be the tutor of his son Arthur, Prince of Wales. He wrote a life of Henry VII, giving a very positive account of the King's reign.

**Argentine, Dr John d. 1507** Dr Argentine, educated at Cambridge, was the physician of Edward V and his brother, Richard of Shrewsbury, Duke of York. In his later recollections of the two boys he claimed that Edward, imprisoned in the Tower, feared that he was facing imminent death and prayed daily.

**Anne of Beaujeu 3 April 1461 - 14 November 1522** Anne was Regent of France for her brother, Charles VIII, during the period 1483 to 1491. During 1484, Anne welcomed Henry Tudor and his uncle, Jasper Tudor, Earl of Pembroke, when they fled Brittany. Anne's government lent Henry 40,000 livres tournois to finance his invasion. Later, Anne signed the Treaty of Etaples in 1491 that ended the Hundred Years' War between England and France.

**Anne of Bohemia, Queen of England, 11 May 1366 – 7 June 1394** Anne was the beloved first wife of Richard II. She is buried beside him in Westminster Abbey. On Anne's death, Richard was so distraught by his loss that he set fire to the Palace of Sheen where she had died. He then married a princess of France, who was too young to cohabit, reducing his chances of having a child to succeed him. He therefore named his nephew, Edmund Mortimer, as his heir.

**Anne of Brittany, Duchess of Brittany and Queen of France 25 January 1477 – 9 January 1514** Anne was the eldest daughter and heir of Francis, 2nd Duke of Brittany, who sheltered Henry Tudor during his exile. Edward IV negotiated for a marriage between Anne and his son, Edward, Prince of Wales, but the match was not completed. Anne was married under duress to Charles VIII of France, who sought to annex her independent duchy to France. This, together with Charles' harbouring of Perkin Warbeck, provoked Henry VII to take an army into France. France, which had other interests, notably pursuing claims in Italy, entered into the Treaty of Etaples to negate the English threat. Anne was subsequently obliged to marry Charles's heir, Louis XII.

**Anne of Burgundy, Duchess of Bedford 30 September 1404 – 14 November 1432** Anne was the sister of Philip the Good, Duke of Burgundy, England's ally in the Hundred Years' War. She was married to John of Lancaster, Duke of Bedford and brother of Henry V. The marriage, which took place at Troyes in June 1423, was short, but happy. Anne died of plague in Paris and is buried there. Anne had no children. Her widower's swift remarriage to Jacquetta of Luxembourg caused a rift between England and Burgundy, which the French exploited.

**Anne of York, Duchess of Exeter, 10 August 1439 – 14 January 1476** Anne was the oldest daughter of Richard, Duke of York, and his wife Cecily Neville. She was married to her father's ward, Henry Holland, 3rd Duke of Exeter, in 1445. Exeter supported Lancaster throughout the war and he and Anne had their marriage annulled in 1472. Anne had one daughter by Exeter, Anne Holland. Her second marriage was to Sir Thomas St Leger, who took part in Buckingham's rebellion against Richard III, but Anne was long dead by that time.

**Anne of York, Princess of England 2 November 1475 – 23 November 1511** Anne was the third daughter of Edward IV and Elizabeth Woodville. In early childhood she was betrothed to Philip the Fair, Duke of Burgundy, but the marriage never took place. In 1484, a marriage was arranged for her with Lord Thomas Howard, but this did not happen. The Howards supported Richard III and it took some time for the family to be rehabilitated following the Battle of Bosworth. Anne did marry Howard eventually and became Countess of Surrey. She had four children, but none survived infancy.

**Anthony, Bastard of Burgundy 1421 – 5 May 1504** Anthony was the illegitimate son of Philip the Good, Duke of Burgundy and thus half-brother to Anne, Duchess of Bedford, and Charles the Bold, Duke of Burgundy. In 1467 he visited the English court where he was treated with great honour. The purpose of this was to demonstrate Edward IV's eagerness for a treaty with Burgundy rather than with France. Anthony lived a life that exemplified the romantic tales of the period – a great jouster, a fine soldier, a collector of literature and the lover of many women.

**Arthur, Prince of Wales 20 September 1486 – 2 April 1502** Arthur was the firstborn child of Henry VII and Elizabeth of York. His birth was intended to cement peace between Lancaster and York. The name Arthur was chosen to reflect Henry VII's desire to promote his alleged ancestry from King Arthur. Arthur was designated as Prince of Wales and sent to Ludlow Castle to preside over the Council of the Marches. As he was only a child, authority was wielded by his uncle, Jasper Tudor, Duke of Bedford. In November 1501, Arthur was married to the Spanish Princess, Katherine of Aragon, but died within 6 months of his wedding to the grief of his parents and the whole country.

**Arthurton, George** Originally in the household of Queen Catherine de Valois, he became the confessor of Henry VI.

**Aspall, Robert** Tutor and chaplain of Edmund, Earl of Rutland, he was by the Earl's side when the 17-year-old was stabbed by Lord Clifford following the Battle of Wakefield.

**Asteley, Joan** Head nurse for Henry VI during his childhood.

**Atwater, John, Mayor of Cork** Atwater was a merchant in the city of Cork, who had twice been chosen as Lord Mayor of the city. A convinced Yorkist, he was one of the early initiators of the scheme to put forward Perkin Warbeck as Richard of Shrewsbury, Duke of York. On 16 November 1498, Atwater was tried at Westminster along with Warbeck and others, found guilty and hanged, drawn and quartered at Tyburn.

**Aiscough, William, Bishop of Salisbury d. 29 June 1450** Aiscough was Henry VI's confessor and conducted the marriage ceremony between Henry and Margaret of Anjou. He was murdered by the mob during Jack Cade's rebellion.

# B

**Beauchamp, Lady Anne, Countess of Warwick, 13 July 1426 – 20 September 1492** Anne, who was Countess of Warwick in her own right, was married to Richard Neville, son of the Earl of Salisbury, who adopted the title of Earl of Warwick. Warwick was an adherent of York, until he quarrelled with his cousin, Edward IV, largely because of Edward's marriage to Elizabeth Woodville. Warwick then entered into negotiations with Margaret of Anjou, for the restoration of Henry VI. Anne travelled to France with Warwick and her daughter, also named Anne, who was to be married to Edward of Lancaster, Prince of Wales. When the Lancastrians were defeated at Tewkesbury, Countess Anne was obliged to retire to a convent. Her elder daughter, Isabel, was already married to George, Duke of Clarence, brother of Edward IV, and now her younger daughter, the widowed Anne, was married to Richard, Duke of Gloucester, Edward IV's other brother. The two brothers fought over the inheritance of the sisters and Countess Anne was deprived of her lands and treated as though she were 'naturally dead'. On the accession of Henry VII, some of her lands were restored to her, on the understanding that she would bequeath them to Henry, rather than her grandson Edward, Earl of Warwick.

**Beauchamp, Lady Eleanor, Duchess of Somerset, c. 1405 – 6 March 1467** Wife of Edmund Beaufort, 2nd Duke of Somerset and mother of Henry, 3rd Duke of Somerset, Eleanor was the daughter of Richard Beauchamp, 13th Earl of Warwick and disputed the inheritance by her half-sister, Anne Beauchamp, of the earldom. This was another bone of contention between Somerset and York, as York's ally and nephew by marriage, Richard Neville, was married to the said Anne Beauchamp, Countess of Warwick.

**Beauchamp of Bletsoe, Margaret, Duchess of Somerset, 1410 – 8 August 1472** Married as her second husband John, 1st Duke of Somerset and was the mother of Lady Margaret Beaufort, Countess of Richmond. Her third marriage was to Lionel, Lord Welles, another Lancastrian, who was killed at the Battle of Towton.

**Beauchamp, Richard, 13th Earl of Warwick January, 1382 – 30 April 1439** Warwick was responsible for the upbringing and education of Henry VI from the time that the King was six years old. Warwick was famous as an honourable and chivalrous knight. After three years, Warwick was obliged to request the Regency Council to protect him from any 'grouch' that the King might form against him as a result of proper correction. In 1437, when it was considered that Henry had completed his education, Warwick was sent to Normandy as Lieutenant.

**Beauchamp, Richard, Bishop of Salisbury d.1481** Beauchamp was the son of Sir Walter Beauchamp, Speaker of the House of Commons. He was Chancellor of the Order of the Garter. Following the

Battle of Towton in March 1461, he wrote in despair that the English deserved pity *'even from the French.'*

**Beauchamp, Sir Walter d. 1 January 1430** Formerly Speaker of the House of Commons, Beauchamp was appointed to the household of Catherine de Valois, and subsequently to that of Henry VI. He became Treasurer of the Royal Household and Master of the Horse.

 **Beaufort, Edmund, 2ⁿᵈ Duke of Somerset & Count of Mortain 1406 – 22 May 1455** Beaufort was the grandson of John of Gaunt, Duke of Lancaster. During the 1420s it was rumoured that Beaufort was engaged in an illicit relationship with the Dowager Queen, Catherine de Valois. In order to prevent Beaufort marrying the Queen, an act was passed by Parliament, under the guidance of Humphrey, Duke of Gloucester, Beaufort's rival, to prevent widowed Queens marrying without the consent of their adult sons. Beaufort inherited the dukedom of Somerset in 1448, from his brother John. In 1449, he became Lieutenant of the King's forces in France, replacing Richard, Duke of York. This led to a rift between the two men, especially as Somerset had little success. He disgraced himself by abandoning his troops when the city of Rouen finally fell on 29 October 1449. Despite this, he remained in favour with his cousin, Henry VI, was on good terms with the new Queen, Margaret of Anjou, and had a leading part in the government. By 1450 Somerset and York were close to open war. Threatened by York's men, Somerset retreated to the Tower for safety, but then emerged to retake control of government. When York became Protector, during Henry VI's illness, Somerset was sent to the Tower, where he remained until Henry VI regained his senses. Somerset was killed at the first battle of the Wars of the Roses, at St Albans.

 **Beaufort, Edmund 4ᵗʰ Duke of Somerset, c. 1438 – 6 May 1471** Younger brother of Henry, 3ʳᵈ Duke of Somerset,

Somerset led the Lancastrians at Tewkesbury. Whether his military judgement was poor, or he was unenthusiastic about the Lancastrian cause or for some other, unknown reason, he retreated from a commanding position, making the Lancastrian defeat inevitable. He survived the battle, but was dragged with the other Lancastrian leaders from sanctuary in Tewkesbury Abbey and executed.

**Beaufort, Henry Cardinal, Bishop of Winchester, c. 1475 – 11 April 1447** The second son of John of Gaunt by his third wife, Katherine Swynford, Beaufort was one of the most important members of the Regency Council which governed on behalf of his great-nephew, the infant Henry VI. Beaufort was Chancellor from 1424 to 1426 but was on bad terms with his nephew, Humphrey, Duke of Gloucester, who sought to become Regent rather than just a member of the Council. One of the elements of discord was Beaufort's support of the peace party which sought to end the Hundred Years' War, whereas Gloucester was in favour of pursuing further military campaigns. Created a Cardinal in 1426, Beaufort was one of the judges at the trial of Joan of Arc and witnessed her death.

**Beaufort, Henry, 3rd Duke of Somerset, 26 January 1436 – 15 May 1464** Son of Edmund, 2nd Duke of Somerset, and Lady Eleanor Beauchamp, Beaufort inherited the dukedom on his father's death at St Albans. He, too, was present at that battle and was severely wounded. This loss bred a desire for revenge in Beaufort which King Henry, or his advisers, tried to ameliorate by arranging a Council of Reconciliation in 1457. Unfortunately, both the Yorkists and the Lancastrians, as represented by Somerset, turned up with large bodies of retainers. It was agreed that the Yorkists would pay compensation to Somerset. The other Lords whose fathers had been killed at St Albans and their former enemies were required to walk through the streets of London in what became known as the Loveday procession. Somerset was paired with Richard Neville, Earl of Salisbury. Unfortunately, peace was not to be found. Somerset was one of the chief Lancastrian commanders at the Battle of Towton, which took place on 29 March 1461. Towton was a stunning victory for the Yorkists and Somerset was exiled. He was captured in 1462 after entering Bamburgh in an attempt to support the Lancastrians holding out there. The new King, Edward IV, made every attempt at reconciliation with Somerset and appears to have become genuinely attached to him. It must have therefore been a bitter blow for Edward IV when Somerset was unable to renounce his allegiance to Lancaster and fought for Henry VI at Edgeley More and Hexham. Captured at Hexham on 14 May 1464, he was executed the next day.

**Beaufort, Joan, Queen of Scots, 1404 – 15 July 1445** Granddaughter of John of Gaunt and his third wife, Katherine Swynford, she was married to King James I of Scotland, as part of the negotiation that freed King James from captivity in England. She had eight children by James, and acted as Regent for her son James II after her husband's assassination. She married a second time and had three further children.

**Beaufort, John, 1st Duke of Somerset, 25 March 1403 – 27 May 1444** Son of John, 1st Earl of Somerset and grandson of John of Gaunt, Duke of Lancaster, he inherited the earldom when he was about seven years old. In around 1420 he became involved in his first military expedition in France at which he was captured. He was held prisoner for some 17 years before his ransom was finally paid. On his return he swiftly married Margaret Beauchamp of Bletsoe, by whom he had a daughter, Margaret. In 1442, promoted to the rank of Duke, he led another military expedition to France, which the King's lieutenant there, Richard, Duke of York, felt undermined his own role. Somerset was no more successful in this expedition than he had been in his first. He returned in disgrace and died shortly thereafter, possibly of suicide.

**Beaufort, Lady Margaret Countess of Richmond, 31 May 1443 – 29 June 1509** Daughter of John, 1st Duke of Somerset, Lady Margaret was married at the age of about 12 to Edmund Tudor, Earl of Richmond, half-brother of Henry VI. She was widowed and a mother within 18 months. Her second marriage was to Sir Henry Stafford, a younger son of the Lancastrian, Humphrey, 1st Duke of Buckingham. Stafford fought for Lancaster at Towton, but then swore allegiance to Edward IV. Margaret's son, Henry, was put in the care of the Yorkist William Herbert. Margaret was widowed again for a second time when Stafford died at the Battle of Barnet, fighting for York. Margaret then married Lord Thomas Stanley, an adherent of Edward IV. During the second part of Edward IV's reign, Margaret attempted to have her son Henry Tudor, now in exile in Brittany, rehabilitated, and possibly married to Edward IV's daughter, Elizabeth. When Richard III became King, Margaret, a well-known figure at court, attended his wife at the coronation. However, Margaret was working behind-the-scenes to support an invasion by her son. On Henry's victory at the Battle of Bosworth, 22 August 1485, Margaret assumed a position of power and influence until her death in 1509.

**Beaufort, Thomas, Duke of Exeter, c. 1377 – 31 December 1426** The third son of John of Gaunt, Duke of Lancaster, and his third wife, Katherine Swynford, Exeter was Lieutenant of Normandy during Henry V's reign. He was a negotiator at the Treaty of Troyes, which arranged the marriage of Henry V to Catherine de Valois, and agreed that Henry V would inherit his father-in-law, Charles VI's, kingdom. Captured at the Battle of Bauge in 1421, he was released in 1422 and acted as executor of the will of Henry V. He was given overall responsibility for the governance of Henry VI's person and was responsible for choosing his household.

**Beaumont, John, 1st Viscount Beaumont, Constable of England c. 1409 – 10 July 1460** Beaumont was a member of Henry VI's Council and became Constable of England in 1445. He was also steward of the Duchy of Lancaster, the King's personal estate. He was one of the Lords commissioned to suppress Jack Cade's rebellion in 1450. During York's first Protectorate (March 1453 – January 1454) Beaumont was a member of his Council. Despite his marriage to Katherine Neville, Dowager Duchess of Norfolk, who was the sister York's Duchess, Cecily, Beaumont remained firmly loyal to Henry VI. In 1459 he was one of the Lords who worked with Margaret of Anjou to achieve the attainder of the Yorkist Lords. In 1460 he was killed at the Battle of Northampton, a Yorkist victory.

**Beaumont, William, 2nd Viscount Beaumont April 1438 – 19 December 1507** William Beaumont fought alongside his father for Lancaster at the Battle of Northampton in 1460, following which he inherited his father's title and estates. He was also in the Lancastrian army at Towton and following the Yorkist victory was attainted and stripped of his titles and lands. Like many other Lancastrians he received a pardon from Edward IV but his lands were not returned. Unreconciled he continued to support Lancastrian rear-guard actions. He was taken prisoner and held at Hammes by Sir James Blount, the Yorkist captain of Calais. When Blount switched sides, Beaumont was released and joined Henry Tudor in Brittany. He was part of the invasion fleet and subsequent victory by Henry at Bosworth. He was restored in titles and lands in the Parliament of November 1485. In later life he appears to have suffered some sort of mental illness, and was confined to the care of his old colleague, John de Vere, 13th Earl of Oxford.

**Bernard VII, Count of Armagnac 1360 – 12 June 1418**  Bernard was the father-in-law of Charles of Orleans, who, when his father, Louis of Orleans, was assassinated by Philip the Bold, Duke of Burgundy, built an alliance with Bernard to take control of the government of Charles' uncle, the incapacitated Charles VI of France.  The feud between the Burgundians and the Armagnacs was a byword for savagery.  The alliance of the Burgundians with the English enabled the victories of Henry V in the early 15th century.

**Bourchier, John, 1st Baron Berners d. May 1474**  Lord Berners was Constable of Windsor Castle and a member of Henry VI's Council. He was present, on the Lancastrian side, at the first Battle of St Albans, but was unharmed.

Boteler, Ralph, 1st Baron Sudeley, c 1394 – 2 May 1473 A Lancastrian supporter, and Treasurer of England.

**Bettini, de Sforza, Milanese Ambassador to Louis XI d. after 31 August 1497**  Probably a relative of the Sforza Dukes of Milan, de Bettini was sent as ambassador to France in around 1467.  He sent a number of reports about happenings in England to his master, including the information that Edward of York was unlikely to regain his throne after having been ousted by Warwick.  As it happens he had been misinformed and he later complained that it was almost impossible to find out the truth of what was happening in England.  He later became a servant of Lorenzo the Magnificent, the ruler of Florence, and, after Lorenzo's death disappeared into gaol in 1497, never to be seen again.

**Blacman, John**  Blacman was Henry VI's confessor, and wrote a memoir about his former master.  Blacman emphasised Henry's humility, religious faith and simplicity.

**Blake, Thomas**  In 1477, Thomas Blake, together with John Stacey and Thomas Burdet, were arrested on a charge of attempting to foresee the King's death by means of sorcery.  Blake was pardoned, whilst the other two were hanged.

**Blount, Sir William c. 1449 - 4 April 1471**  Blount was an ally of Edward IV, killed at the Battle of Barnet.

**Boleyn, Anne, Queen of England c. 1503 – 1536**  Anne, daughter of one of Henry VIII's courtiers, spent her formative years in France, before joining the English court as one of Queen Katherine's maids-of-honour in 1521.  It is not known for certain when Anne caught Henry's eye, but sometime during the period 1525-6 he fell violently in love with her.  This passion coincided with his fears for the succession as Queen Katherine was past childbearing and they had only a daughter.  Henry decided, contrary to all custom, that he wanted to marry Anne Boleyn, she having refused to be his mistress.

Anne's experience at the French court had introduced her to modern religious thought, and she was seen as a religious reformer.  Wolsey was unable to arrange for Henry's marriage to be annulled and Anne, working with Cromwell and Cranmer, was involved in the steps taken to divide the English Church from Rome.  Anne was crowned in 1533, but the fact that she failed to produce the son whom Henry so much desired led him to question the marriage.  Anne was charged with adultery and incest, tried, convicted and executed within a month.

**Bonville, Sir William, 1st Baron Bonville c. 30 August 1393 – 17 February 1461**  The clash between the Bonvilles and Courtenays for pre-eminence in Devon was one of the long-running noble feuds that contributed to the Wars of the

Roses. Bonville fought for York at the Battle of Northampton where Henry VI was captured. Bonville was holding the King at the Battle of St Albans, when the Yorkists were defeated. He was executed immediately after the battle.

**Bourchier, Henry, 1st Earl of Essex c. 1404 – 4 April 1483** A descendant of Edward III through his mother, Anne of Gloucester, in his early days Bourchier fought in France and was created a baron in 1445. He supported York, who was the brother of Bourchier's wife, Isabel, at the 2nd Battle of St Albans and Edward of York at Towton. Following that Yorkist victory, he was granted the earldom of Essex by the new King, Edward IV. He served Edward as Lord High Treasurer, and attended the coronation of Queen Elizabeth Woodville.

**Bourchier, Humphrey, Lord Cromwell d. 14 April 1471** Son of Henry Bourchier, 1st Earl of Essex and first cousin of Edward IV, he was Lord Cromwell in right of his wife, Joan Cromwell. He was killed fighting for York at the Battle of Tewkesbury.

**Bourchier, Thomas Archbishop of Canterbury c. 1405 – 30 March 1486** A descendant of Edward III through his mother, Anne of Gloucester. Educated at Oxford he entered the Church, became Bishop of Worcester, Chancellor of the University of Oxford, Bishop of Ely and finally, in 1454, Archbishop of Canterbury. As was common, he combined the latter post with the position of Lord Chancellor. By 1459, Bourchier was beginning to favour York and he was present with the Yorkist army at the Battle of Northampton. In 1483, Bourchier, now a Cardinal, persuaded Elizabeth Woodville to release her younger son, Richard of Shrewsbury, Duke of York, to the care of his uncle, now crowned Richard III, by Bourchier. Bourchier presided at the coronation of Henry VII and married the King to Elizabeth of York.

**Bourchier, Sir Thomas d. 1492**   Suspected of plotting against Richard III, he was imprisoned in the Tower in 1483. Whilst being moved to another location, he and Sir Walter Hungerford escaped and joined Henry Tudor's army at Bosworth.

**Bouttiler, Dame Alice**   Henry VI's governess. (Dame was a title used to refer to a knight's widow. During her husband's lifetime she would be named Lady.)

**Brackenbury, Sir Robert d.22 August 1485**   Brackenbury was Treasurer of Richard III's household when the latter was still Duke of Gloucester. On 17 July 1483 he was appointed as Constable of the Tower of London. He was in the front line at the Battle of Bosworth, where he was killed.

**Brandon, Sir William 1456 – 22 August 1485**   Brandon, a native of East Anglia, appears to have led rather a wild life in his youth. He was arrested for rape but either was not convicted or was pardoned. He joined in Buckingham's rebellion against Richard III. He was pardoned for this but left for France and was involved in the relief of the siege of Hammes. He joined Henry Tudor in Brittany and was part of the invasion force. He was killed at the Battle of Bosworth where he acted as Henry's standard-bearer. His son, Charles, Duke of Suffolk, was the second husband of Henry VII's daughter, Mary, the French Queen.

**Bray, Reginald c. 1440 - 24 June 1503**   Bray was a member of the household of Sir Henry Stafford, husband of Lady Margaret Beaufort, Countess of Richmond. He remained in her service following the death of Stafford, and was a go-between for the Countess with Henry Stafford, 2nd Duke of Buckingham in connection with Buckingham's rebellion against Richard III in 1483. Attainted for his part in the rebellion, he escaped to France where he joined Lady Margaret's son, Henry Tudor, in

Brittany.    Once Henry became King, Bray became Chancellor of the Duchy of Lancaster and was one of Henry's most trusted councillors, acting as executor of his will.

**Bridget of York 10 November 1480-1517**  Bridget was the youngest child of Edward IV and Elizabeth Woodville.  She was carried to her christening by Lady Margaret Beaufort, Countess of Richmond.  She became a nun at Dartford Priory, dying in 1517.

**Brotherman, Margaret**  Laundress in the household of Henry VI, when he was a child.

**Burdet, Thomas d. 19 May 1477**  Burdet was a servant of George, Duke of Clarence, and was arrested, together with John Stacey and Thomas Blake, for attempting to foretell, by sorcery, the death of the King.  He was found guilty, and hanged at Tyburn.    Shortly thereafter the Duke of Clarence announced the innocence of the men during a Council meeting.

**Bureau, Jean**  Bureau commanded the cavalry at the Battle of Castillon on 17 July 1453, annihilating the English army under Sir John Talbot, Earl of Shrewsbury.  The shock of this defeat precipitated Henry VI's descent into mental illness.

**Burgh, Sir Thomas, of Gainsborough c. 1430 - 18 March 1496**  Burgh was a bodyguard and close associate of Edward IV.  During 1470, a private feud with Richard, Lord Welles led to a battle between Edward IV and allies of the Earl of Warwick.

**Burgh, Walter de**  A Londoner who accused Sir William Oldhall, Chamberlain to Richard, Duke of York and formerly a speaker of the House of Commons, of looting the goods of Edmund Beaufort, 2nd Duke of Somerset. He was attacked in the street, which Somerset believed was on the orders of Oldhall, who he had dragged from sanctuary in response to the attack

**Butler, Lady Eleanor nee Talbot c. 1436 - 30 June 1468** The daughter of Sir John Talbot, Earl of Shrewsbury, and Margaret Beauchamp (sister of Eleanor Beauchamp, Duchess of Somerset), Lady Eleanor was married at the age of 13 to Sir Thomas Butler who died sometime before 4 March 1461. In 1483, Richard, Duke of Gloucester, claimed that Lady Eleanor had been secretly married to his brother, Edward IV, and that therefore Edward's subsequent marriage to Elizabeth Woodville was invalid, making his children by Elizabeth, including Edward V, illegitimate.

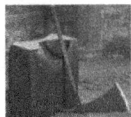

**Butler, James, Earl of Ormond and Wiltshire 24 November 1420 – 1 May 1461** Ormond, initially an associate of the Duke of York, married Somerset's daughter, Lady Eleanor Beaufort, in around 1458. He was given the position Lieutenant of Ireland, when York was relieved of that post. He fought for Lancaster at the Battle of Mortimer's Cross on 2 February 1461, and again at Towton. Following Towton he was executed by the victorious Yorkists. At one time he was described as the best looking man in the kingdom.

# C

**Cade, Jack. d. 16 July 1450** Cade was the leader of the rebellion which began in Kent in the early summer of 1450. Whilst there is no evidence at all that Cade had any relationship with the Duke of York, one of his demands was that York should be recalled from Ireland and involved in royal government. Cade's men arrived at Blackheath in mid-June, and after a number of skirmishes Henry VI and his government left

London.   The rebels executed without trial a number of Henry VI's advisers.   Queen Margaret issued a proclamation offering pardons to rebels who would return home.   Cade refused, was denounced as a traitor and captured in Sussex in action during which he was mortally wounded.

**Calot, Lawrence**   Calot was one of the clerks of John of Lancaster, Duke of Bedford.   He wrote a detailed claim of Henry VI's right to the French throne, which was based not just on his father's victories and the Treaty of Troyes, but also on his hereditary rights.

**Catherine de Valois, Queen of England, 27 October 1401 – 3 January 1437**   Catherine was the youngest daughter of Charles VI of France and Isabeau of Bavaria.   By the Treaty of Troyes, Catherine was married in June 1422 to Henry V, King of England, and now heir apparent to her father.   Within two years Catherine was a widow and mother of an infant King.   During his early childhood she was always with him, but when Henry VI reached the age of about eight, as was customary, he left the care of his mother, to be brought up by men. Catherine was suspected of planning to marry Edmund Beaufort, brother of the Duke of Somerset.   An act was quickly rushed through Parliament to prevent widowed Queens marrying without the consent of their adult sons.   Catherine however ignored this and married Owen Tudor, a member of her household.   They had several children before Catherine died, after a long illness, at Bermondsey Abbey.

 **Catesby, Sir William, c. 1450 – 25 August 1485**   A faithful supporter of Richard III, he was Speaker of the House of Commons in the Parliament of 1484.   Captured at the Battle of Bosworth, he was executed three days later.

**Caxton, William. c.1422 – 1491**   In around 1475, Caxton brought the first printing press to England.   He was patronised by Edward IV's brother-in-law, Anthony, Earl Rivers.

**Cecily of York 20 March 1469 – 24 August 1507** Cecily was the second daughter of Edward IV and Elizabeth of York. She was married to John, 1st Viscount Welles, stepbrother of Lady Margaret Beaufort, Countess of Richmond. The marriage was part of Henry VII's efforts to integrate York and Lancaster. Her second marriage, to Thomas Kyme of Lincolnshire, led to her being disgraced and banished from court.

**Chapuys, Eustace c. 1490 – 1556** Chapuys was the ambassador to Henry VIII from Charles V, Holy Roman Emperor. He was resident in England from 1529 to 1545. Much of our knowledge of the court of Henry VIII is based on his letters to Charles V and Charles' sister, Mary of Hungary, who was his Regent in the Low Countries. Chapuys was a strong supporter of Katherine of Aragon and Princess Mary, both personally, and on behalf of his master. Often portrayed as Spanish, he was, in fact, from Savoy, in the Franco-Italian border.

**Charles IV, King of France 19 June 1294 – 1 February 1328** Charles was the father of Isabella of France, and thus the grandfather of Edward III of England. It was through this relationship that England claimed the throne of France.

**Charles V, Holy Roman Emperor, 24 February 1500 – 21 September 1558** Nephew of Katherine of Aragon, first wife of Henry VIII, Charles V was the most powerful man in Europe in the first half of the 16th century. At the Battle of Pavia on 24 February 1525 where Charles defeated François I of France, Richard de la Pole, the last 'White Rose' was killed.

**Charles VI, King of France 3 December 1368 – 21 October 1422** Variously known as Charles the Well Beloved or Charles the Mad, he was father both of Isabelle of Valois, the second wife of Richard II, and also of Catherine of Valois, the wife of Henry V. King Charles' mental incapacity meant that his kingdom was completely vulnerable to the onslaughts of the English.   The argument between his brother, Louis of Orleans (Armagnacs) and his uncle, Philip the Good, Duke of Burgundy (Burgundians) as to who should rule on his behalf fatally weakened his kingdom. He (or his government) agreed in the Treaty of Troyes, signed on 21st May 1420, that Henry V of England would marry his daughter, Catherine, and inherit his kingdom.  Charles died within 6 months of the Treaty being agreed.

**Charles VII, King of France, 22 January 1403 – 22 July 1461**
The son of Charles VI, he refused to accept the Treaty of Troyes and continued to resist English dominance in France.  The advent of Joan of Arc completely transformed his fortunes and he went on to drive the English out of his country.  His wife, Marie of Anjou, was the aunt of Margaret of Anjou, Queen of England.  The marriage treaty between Charles VII and Henry VI resulted in the ceding of Maine to France.  This was bitterly disliked by many of Henry VI's nobles, and made Margaret unpopular from the first day of her arrival in England.

**Charles VIII, King of France 30 June 1470 – 7 April 1498**  The son of Louis XI of France, Charles inherited the throne at the age of 13. His sister, Anne of Beaujeu, acted as Regent.  They supported the invasion of England by Henry Tudor, but when Charles attempted to annex the Duchy of Brittany and also showed support for the pretender, Perkin Warbeck, he was obliged to face Henry's army.  More interested in his claims to territory in Italy, than in reigniting the Hundred Years War, Charles VIII and Henry VII came to a final agreement at the Treaty of Etaples in 1491.  Charles died, aged 28, when he hit his head on a stone doorway.

**Charles the Bold, Duke of Burgundy, 10 November 1433 – 5 January 1477** Charles married, as his second wife, Margaret of York, sister of Edward IV.  Although initially a supporter of Lancaster, when it appeared that France, Burgundy's enemy, was preparing to support the recapture of the throne by Henry VI, Charles was persuaded to give money and men to his brother-in-law, Edward of York. This resulted in Edward's successful return to England which culminated in the Battle of Tewkesbury.

**Chaucer, Alice, Duchess of Suffolk 1404 – 1475** Alice, who was the granddaughter of the poet Geoffrey Chaucer, and the great-niece of Katherine Swynford, Duchess of Lancaster, married as her second husband Thomas Montacute, 4th Earl of Salisbury. Alice had no children by Salisbury, but by her third husband, William de la Pole, 1st Duke of Suffolk, she had a son, John. John was briefly married as a child to Lady Margaret Beaufort, Countess of Richmond, but their marriage was annulled. He subsequently married Elizabeth of York, daughter of Richard, Duke of York. This encouraged Alice to change her allegiance to York, after the death of Suffolk in 1450. Her grandsons were all claimants to the English crown.

**Cheyne, John c. 1442 – 1492** Cheyne was a supporter of Edward IV, appointed as a Squire of the Body to Queen Elizabeth Woodville in the 1460s. He supported Henry VII at the Battle of Bosworth, where he was in Henry's bodyguard, and after Henry's victory, received the post of Master of the Horse.

**Christmas, Stephen** Leader of a failed uprising against Henry VI, quashed by the Duke of Somerset.

**Clifford, John, 9th Baron Clifford 8 April 1435 – 28 March 1461** Lord Clifford's father had been killed by the Yorkists at the first Battle of St Albans. He was desperate for revenge and in February 1458 requested compensation for his father's death. Clifford was one of the commanders of Lancastrian forces at Battle of Wakefield where he captured Edmund, Earl of Rutland, the 17-

year-old son of the Duke of York. In an act which was considered barbarous not only by the Yorkists but also by his own side, Clifford stabbed Rutland to death. He was himself killed only three months later at an ambush prior to the Battle of Towton.

**Clifford, Sir Robert, d. 1508** Clifford was a younger son of Thomas, 8th Lord Clifford, but unlike his brother, John, 9th Lord Clifford, appears to have been reconciled to York. He became involved in the attempts to identify Perkin Warbeck as Richard of Shrewsbury Duke of York, and was sent by various interested parties to Flanders to check the young man's identity. Clifford (who may have been a double agent) denounced Sir William Stanley as implicated in the affair.

**Clifford Thomas, 8th Lord Clifford, 25 March 1414 – 22 May 1455** Clifford had taken part in military manoeuvres in France with John of Lancaster, Duke of Bedford, during the 1430s. He was a loyal supporter of Lancaster and one of the commanders of the King's troops at the first Battle of St Albans. He was killed during the battle.

**Cobham, Reginald, 3rd Lord Cobham** As the father of Eleanor Cobham, Duchess of Gloucester, he was one of the earliest adherents of the Duke of York's party.

**Cobham, Eleanor, Duchess of Gloucester, c. 1400 – 7 July 1452** Eleanor was a lady-in-waiting to Jacqueline of Hainault, Duchess of Gloucester, but soon became the mistress of the Duke. When the Duke's marriage was annulled in 1425, he married Eleanor. Eleanor was convicted of witchcraft, when it came to light that she had consulted astrologers with regard to the King's health. She was required to do public penance, her marriage was annulled and she was imprisoned in various castles and finally at Beaumaris in Anglesey where she died.

**Commines, Philip de 1447 – 18 October 1511**  Commines was initially in the service of Charles the Bold, Duke of Burgundy, but in 1472 he left Burgundy by stealth to join the court of Charles's great enemy, Louis XI of France.  He wrote a memoir on which much of our knowledge of the period is based.

**Conyers, Sir John of Hornby d. 1490**  Conyers was a retainer first of Richard Neville, Earl of Salisbury, and secondly of Salisbury's son, Richard Neville, Earl of Warwick.  He fought for York at Blore Heath but his loyalty was to his own lord and he supported Warwick's insurrection against Edward IV.  He may have been the outlaw Robin of Redesdale or he may have used Robin's name in a second uprising planned by Warwick.  He was later retained by Richard III, for whom he fought at Bosworth.  He survived and later supported Henry VII at the Battle of Stoke.  Conyers had a son of the same name, who followed a similar career path.

**Cooke, Sir Thomas.**  Cooke was a Draper who became Lord Mayor of London in 1462 to 1463.  He had lent significant sums of money to Edward IV.  In 1468 he was accused, together with other London aldermen, of plotting against King Edward.  He was tried and acquitted of treason but found guilty of 'misprision' of treason – that is, knowing of treasonable activity and not reporting it.  He received a heavy fine, but was pardoned.

**Courtenay, Sir Edward, 1st Earl of Devon d. 1509**  Son of Sir Hugh Courtenay, following the usurpation of Richard III, he carried messages between Lady Margaret Beaufort, Countess of Richmond, and her son in exile, Henry Tudor.  When Henry took the throne as Henry VII, the title of Earl of Devon was recreated for him.  He supported Henry VII against Perkin Warbeck.

**Courtenay, Henry, Marquess of Exeter c. 1498 – 1538** Courtenay was the son of Henry VIII's aunt, Katherine of York, and spent much of his childhood in the royal nurseries with Henry VIII, Margaret, Queen of Scots, and Mary the French Queen. Nevertheless, his childhood was overshadowed by the imprisonment of his father and grandfather for alleged Yorkist conspiracies. Following Henry VIII's accession, Courtenay was permitted to inherit the title of Earl of Devon, and he served in the French wars of 1512-13 in the English navy. He grew close to his cousin, the King, and was appointed to the Privy Council in 1520. In 1525, he received the title of Marquess of Exeter. Exeter supported Henry in his annulment proceedings, but, no supporter of Anne Boleyn, he collaborated in her downfall. In 1538, Exeter was accused of conspiring with his cousins, Reginald Pole and Henry Pole, Lord Montague to restore Papal authority, and possibly replace Henry himself. Exeter, Montague and others were attainted and executed.

**Courtenay, Sir Hugh, c.1427 - 4 May 1471** Cousin of the earls of Devon he joined the Lancastrian army of Margaret of Anjou and fought at Tewkesbury. Following defeat he sought sanctuary in the Abbey, but, together with the Duke of Somerset and a number of others, he was dragged out and tried in a court assembled in front of Richard of Gloucester, Constable of England. Courtenay and the others were executed.

**Courtenay, Sir John, c. 1435 - 4 May 1471** His older brother, Thomas, 14th Earl of Devon, having been executed, in Lancastrian eyes Sir John became the 15th Earl. As the 14th Earl had been attainted by Yorkist Parliament, this was not of much practical use. In 1471, Courtenay joined the invasion force of Margaret of Anjou and was killed at the Battle of Tewkesbury.

**Courtenay, Peter, Bishop of Exeter c. 1432 - 23 September 1492**
A distant cousin of the Earl of Devon, Courtenay received a number of
ecclesiastical benefices under Edward IV. He became involved in the
rebellion of the Duke of Buckingham against Richard III and when that
collapsed escaped to France, where he joined Henry Tudor. He became
Keeper of the Privy Seal, assisted at Henry VII's coronation and at the
investiture of Henry's son, Arthur, as Prince of Wales.

**Courtenay, Thomas, 13th Earl of Devon, 1414 – 3 February 1458**
Devon was married as a young man to Margaret Beaufort, daughter of
John, 1st Earl of Somerset and aunt of John, 1st Duke and Edmund, 2nd
Duke of Somerset. Nevertheless he became attached to Richard, Duke of
York's party. His private feud with his rivals for influence in Devon and
Cornwall, the Bonvilles, was a contributing factor to the unrest which
bedevilled Henry VI's reign. Quarrels with the Bonvilles resulted in
Devon's arrest and imprisonment. Following this, his relationship with
York cooled as York appeared to favour the Bonvilles. Devon was present
for Lancaster at the Battle of St Albans, where he was lightly wounded.
He died of natural causes in 1458.

**Courtenay, Thomas, 14th Earl of Devon, 1432 – 3
April 1461** Devon, as closely involved as his father, the 13th
Earl, in the feuding with the Bonvilles, fought for Lancaster
at Towton. Captured during the battle, he was executed immediately
after. He was attainted by Parliament and his goods and titles forfeit.

**Courtenay, William 2nd Earl of Devon, 1475 - 9 June 1511** Son
and heir of Edward Courtenay, 1st Earl of Devon, he was married to
Katherine of York, sister of Queen Elizabeth of York. For some unknown
reason he supported the claim of Edmund de la Pole, 3rd Duke of Suffolk
to the throne, for which he was attainted and imprisoned. He was
released on the accession of Henry VIII and his title restored.

**Coventry, John, Lord Mayor of London**  Coventry was selected as Lord Mayor of London in October 1425.  The very day of his inaugural feast he was summoned to a meeting with Humphrey, Duke of Gloucester, and told to protect London against a possible attack by troops of Cardinal Beaufort, Bishop of Winchester.

**Crowmer, William, Sheriff of Kent 3 July 1450**  Crowmer was one of the unlucky men taken prisoner by Jack Cade's men during their rebellion in 1450.  He was lynched by the mob.

**Crue Thomas**  Edmund de la Pole, Duke of Suffolk, was accused, in 1498, of murdering a man named Thomas Crue.  This precipitated Suffolk's rebellion against Henry VII.

# D

**Daubeney, Sir Giles, 1 June 1451 – 21 May 1508**  Daubeney was in the army of Edward IV that invaded France in 1475.  He became one of Edward IV's bodyguards and was present at the coronation of Richard III.  He was attainted for his part in the rebellion of the Duke of Buckingham in 1483 but escaped to Brittany where he joined Henry Tudor.  He was present at the Battle of Bosworth and became one of Henry VII's most trusted advisers, a Privy Councillor and leader of the King's forces both against the Scots and against the Cornish rebels.

**Devereux, Sir Walter c. 1431 – 22 August 1485**  The Devereux family were clients of the Duke of York and were rivals in South Wales for prominence against Edmund Tudor, Earl of Richmond.  In the Coventry Parliament of 1460, Devereux was attainted.  Knighted at the Battle of Towton he attained high office under Edward IV.  He survived both the Battles of Barnet and

Tewkesbury and became a councillor of the young Edward, Prince of Wales. He transferred his allegiance to Richard III and died at Bosworth.

**Dudley, Edmund d. 17 August 1510.** Speaker of the House of Commons and a Privy Councillor, Dudley was hated for his effective tax gathering and implementation of some of Henry VII's more unpleasant money raising tactics. On the accession of Henry VIII, he was gaoled and executed.

## Edmund to Isabelle

## E

**Edmund, Earl of Rutland 17 May 1443 – 30 May 1460**  Edmund was the second son of Richard, Duke of York, and his Duchess, Cecily Neville.  Brought up closely with his brother Edward, when the Yorkist Lords fled from Ludlow, Edmund went with his father to Ireland.  He was with York at the Battle of Wakefield.  Following the battle he was captured and deliberately killed, by Lord Clifford, in revenge for the death of Clifford's father at St Albans.  His head was placed next to York's on Mickelgate Bar, overlooking the city of York.  He was later interred at Fotheringhay Castle in an elaborate ceremony commemorating his father and himself.

**Edward II, King of England, 21 April 1284 – 21 September 1327**  Edward, a weak King, had faced a number of rebellions which he had overcome largely with the help and support of his wife, Isabella of France.  When Isabella and her lover, Roger Mortimer, took arms against the King he had no hope of success.  He was deposed, imprisoned, and probably murdered.  Isabella was the daughter of Philip IV of France, and after the death of all of her brothers without direct heirs, her son, Edward III of England, claimed the throne of France.  This gave rise to the Hundred Years' War.

**Edward III, King of England, 13 November 1312 – 21 June 1377**  Edward III, who became King at the age of 14 when his father was deposed by his mother, Isabella, and Roger Mortimer, took power himself three years later.  He claimed the throne of France as the grandson of Philip IV.  It was Edward's proliferation of sons that led to the problem of multiple heirs to the throne and was a contributing factor in the Wars of the Roses.

## Edward IV, King of England, 28 April 1442 – 9 April 1483

Edward was the oldest son of Richard, Duke of York, and his wife, Cecily Neville. Following the Yorkist surrender at Ludford Bridge in 1459, Edward fled with his uncle, Richard Neville, Earl of Salisbury, and his cousin, Richard Neville, Earl of Warwick, to Calais where they raised an army. In 1460 Edward landed in Kent, marched through England and captured Henry VI at the Battle of Northampton. Following his father's death at Wakefield, Edward now Duke of York, fought a successful engagement at Mortimer's Cross. He reached London, where he claimed the Crown, and then marched north to defeat the Lancastrians at the bloody Battle of Towton. Edward made sustained efforts to reconcile Lancastrians to his rule but infighting amongst the Yorkists broke out when his cousin, Warwick, angry that Edward did not always follow his advice, particularly in the matter of his marriage, raised rebellion, together with Edward's brother, George, Duke of Clarence. Although the initial rebellion was overcome, in 1470 Warwick formed an alliance with Margaret of Anjou to reinstate Henry VI. Edward escaped to Burgundy, but returned the following year claiming he wished only to be reconfirmed in his title of Duke of York. He raised an army and finally defeated the Lancastrians at Tewkesbury, following which Henry VI was swiftly dispatched. Although less forgiving than he had been in the earlier part of his reign, Edward IV was a successful and popular king and the vast majority of Lancastrians accepted his rule, particularly as Henry VI's, son, Edward of Lancaster, Prince of Wales, had been killed at Tewkesbury. Edward died at the early age of 40, leaving a son who was a minor.

## Edward V, King of England, 2 November 1470 – probably 1483

Edward V, son of Edward IV and Elizabeth Woodville, became King at the age of 12. He had spent most of his childhood at the castle of Ludlow in the Welsh Marches, as nominal head of the Council of the Marches, under the guardianship of his maternal uncle, Anthony Woodville, Earl Rivers. On his father's death, he set out for London, with a small bodyguard. Intercepted at Stony Stratford, Northampton, by his paternal uncle, Richard, Duke of Gloucester, Edward was obliged to witness the arrest of Earl Rivers and his own half-brother, Sir Richard Grey. Edward was taken to London and lodged in the Tower. In early June it was declared that his parents' marriage was invalid and that he was therefore illegitimate. His uncle took the Crown as Richard III and Edward was last sighted together with his brother, Richard of Shrewsbury, Duke of York, in the summer of 1483.

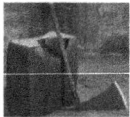

**Edward, Earl of Warwick, 25 February 1475 – 28 November 1498** Edward was the son of George, Duke of Clarence, and the nephew of Edward IV and Richard III. Edward inherited the title of Earl of Warwick and a moiety of the Warwick lands on the death of his mother, Isabel Neville, when he was only a year old. Following his father's execution for treason in 1478, Warwick was brought up with his cousins, the King's younger son and daughters. When Richard III announced that all of the children of Edward IV were illegitimate, Warwick was passed over as the next heir on the basis of his father's attainder. Warwick was sent to Middleham Castle where he probably remained until the accession of Henry VII when, aged only 10, he was sent to the Tower. Unfortunately for Warwick his name was used by both Lambert Simnel and Perkin Warbeck (although the latter later claimed to be Richard of Shrewsbury, Duke of York). Warwick remained in the Tower until, in 1499, he was accused of involvement in a plot to escape with Perkin Warbeck. It is likely that pressure from Ferdinand and Isabella to have this Yorkist claimant removed, encouraged Henry VII to proceed against him. The young man was tried and executed.

**Edward of Lancaster, Prince of Wales, 13 October 1453 – 4 May 1471** Edward was born to Henry VI and Margaret of Anjou after seven years of marriage. His birth occurred during Henry's first period of mental illness, and it was not until the baby was nearly a year old that Henry returned to something like normal mental health. Edward's birth created a problem for the Yorkist party which had been anticipating that on Henry's death York would inherit. In 1460, Edward was disinherited when it was agreed that, whilst Henry VI would continue to reign for the rest of his life, York would take the throne thereafter. Margaret of Anjou never accepted this and, exiled in France, once Edward IV was King, brought Edward up to dream of revenge. In 1470, in a deal with the Earl of Warwick, Edward was married to Warwick's younger daughter, Anne Neville. Edward, his mother, and a large Lancastrian force landed in England, in early 1471, and marched with great haste towards Wales to meet another Lancastrian force under Jasper Tudor, Earl of Pembroke. Their army was caught at Tewkesbury by Edward IV and annihilated. It is not certain whether 17-year-old Edward was killed in battle or killed afterwards by the Yorkist victors.

**Edward of Middleham, Prince of Wales, December 1473 – 9 April 1484** Edward was the only child of Richard III and Anne Neville. He was invested as Prince of Wales at York Minster on 8 September 1483. He died the following April to the great grief of his parents.

**Elizabeth I, 9 September 1533 – 24 March 1603** Elizabeth was the daughter of Henry VIII and Anne Boleyn. Her gender was a terrible disappointment to her parents, who had expected a son, but as Elizabeth grew up she proved to be exceptionally clever and charismatic. Elizabeth succeeded as Queen in 1558, and re-established Royal Supremacy over the English Church. Elizabeth's reign of 45 years, although it was not all plain sailing, is seen as a golden era of exploration, relative (by extremely low sixteenth century standards) religious tolerance and the flowering of English literature.

**Elizabeth of Lancaster, Duchess of Exeter, c. 21 February 1363 – 24 November 1426** Elizabeth was the older sister of Henry IV, the mother of Henry Holland, 2$^{nd}$ Duke of Exeter and grandmother of Henry Holland, 3$^{rd}$ Duke of Exeter, a Lancastrian commander.

**Elizabeth of York, Duchess of Suffolk, 22 April 1444 – 1503/1504** Elizabeth was the second daughter of Richard, Duke of York and his Duchess, Cecily Neville. She was married aged about 14 to John de la Pole, son of the Duke of Suffolk, who was Henry VI's closest adviser. Suffolk had been impeached for bad government and was later lynched. Elizabeth's husband became a firm supporter of her father and later of her brothers, Edward IV and Richard III. Elizabeth had 11 children, of whom the eldest, John, Earl of Lincoln, was possibly named as his heir by Richard III. Following Henry VII's accession, Elizabeth's loyalties were probably torn as her husband supported Henry VII, whilst her oldest son, and later his brothers, claimed the throne.

**Elizabeth of York, Queen of England, 11 February 1466 – 11 February 1503** Elizabeth was the firstborn child of Edward IV and Elizabeth Woodville. When she was four, she retreated with her mother into sanctuary at Westminster Abbey for the short period of Henry VI's readeption. She was betrothed in her youth to the Dauphin of France and the breaking off of the match by the French infuriated her father. When Richard III took the throne, her mother and Lady Margaret Beaufort, Countess of Richmond entered into secret negotiations whereby Elizabeth would marry Lady Margaret's son, Henry Tudor, and thus unite the claims of Lancaster and York. Henry said publicly that if his invasion were successful he would marry Elizabeth or if she were unavailable, one of her sisters. Henry VII gained the crown in August 1485 and he and Elizabeth were married in January 1486. They appear to have been happily married and had seven children. Elizabeth died in childbirth on her 37th birthday, much mourned by her husband and family.

**Empson, Sir Richard c. 1450 – 17 August 1510** Empson was a lawyer and Speaker of the House of Commons. He became notorious for the zeal with which he carried out some of Henry VII's more unpopular money raising strategies. On Henry VII's death he was arrested, imprisoned and executed a year later.

# F

**Fastolf, Sir John, 1380 – 5 November 1459** Fastolf was a commander in France under John of Lancaster, Duke of Bedford. He was the only English captain who survived the Battle of Patay, which followed the raising of the siege of Orleans by Joan of Arc.

**Ferdinand of Aragon, 10 March 1452 – 23 January 1516** By the Treaty of Medina del Campo 1489, Henry VII agreed that his oldest son, Arthur, would marry the daughter of Ferdinand of Aragon and his wife Isabella of Castile. This alliance gave Henry VII international recognition, and the Spanish sovereigns continued to support him when other European rulers were flirting with Perkin Warbeck.

**Fiennes, James, 1st Baron Saye, c. 1395 – 4 July 1450** Saye served as Treasurer to Henry VI and was obliged to find money where it did not exist for the defence of

France. He even resorted to pawning the Crown jewels. An unpopular figure, he was arrested in an attempt to placate Jack Cade's rebels and sent to the Tower. Along with others, he was dragged out and lynched by the mob.

**Fisher, John, Bishop of Rochester, 1469 – 1535** Fisher studied at Cambridge and was ordained in 1491. He became Chaplain and Confessor to Lady Margaret Beaufort, Countess of Richmond, mother of Henry VII, and was also a Privy Councillor. On Henry VIII's accession, he continued as a Privy Councillor, but was never as favoured by him as by Henry VII. When Henry VIII's annulment suit began, Fisher was appointed as one of Queen Katherine's legal counsel, and he defended the validity of the marriage to the uttermost, being one of only a handful who stood against the King. He refused to sign the Oath of Succession, conferring the Crown on the children of Anne Boleyn and was imprisoned, without the benefit of a priest. The Pope, hoping to alleviate his treatment, appointed him a Cardinal, an act which infuriated the King. Fisher was tried for treason, and convicted. He was condemned and sentenced to be hanged, drawn and quartered. Fearing popular discontent at such a brutal end for a much respected man, Henry commuted the sentence to beheading.

**Fitzgerald, Gerald, 8th Earl of Kildare, c. 1456 – 3 September 1513** Appointed Lord Lieutenant of Ireland by Edward IV he remained in position under Henry VII. However Fitzgerald was a Yorkist heart and was present at the crowning of Lambert Simnel as Edward VI in Dublin Cathedral. Forgiven for his part in the Simnel affair, in 1494 he spent a brief period in the Tower when he was captured by Irish enemies and sent to London accused of treason. Henry VII reappointed him as Lord Deputy in which post he continued until his death in 1513.

**FitzHugh, Henry, 3rd Baron FitzHugh, 1363 – 11 January 1425**
A loyal servant of Henry V, and one of the executors of the King's will, Lord FitzHugh was appointed to support Thomas Beaufort, Duke of Exeter, in the Duke's care of the young Henry VI.

**FitzHugh, Henry, 5th Baron Fitzhugh, 1429 – 8 June 1472** Lord FitzHugh was the brother-in-law of Richard Neville, Earl of Warwick. He took part in Warwick's rebellion against Edward IV.

**FitzAlan, William, 16th Earl of Arundel 23 November 1417 – 1487** Arundel was the brother-in-law of Richard Neville, Earl of Warwick, and supported him fighting for both York and Lancaster. He was present at the 'Loveday' celebration intended to reconcile the warring parties in 1458. He was in Warwick's army at the second Battle of St Albans on 26 February 1461. His son Thomas, was married to Margaret Woodville, sister of Queen Elizabeth Woodville. He remained as Warden of the Cinque Ports under Henry VII.

**FitzWilliam, William, 1st Earl of Southampton c. 1490 – 1542** FitzWilliam spent much of his youth at Henry VII's Court as a companion to the young Prince Henry. When the Prince succeeded as Henry VIII, FitzWilliam received several Court positions, including Admiral of the Fleet and, after the downfall of Cromwell, Lord Privy Seal. He maintained his support of Henry VIII, accepting the annulment of the King's marriage and church reforms. However, he was known to be inimical to Anne Boleyn, and was one of the jurors at her trial. Southampton was instrumental in arranging the annulment of Henry VIII's marriage to Anne of Cleves. He was appointed to lead an expedition to Scotland in 1542, but died shortly thereafter.

**Fosbroke, Matilda** Day nurse for the baby Henry VI.

**Frammesley, John**   Leader of a riot, protesting against the Duke of Suffolk's secret removal from London in 1450, following the Duke's impeachment by Parliament.

**Francis II, Duke of Brittany, 23 June 1438 – 9 September 1488**
In September 1471 Jasper Tudor, Earl of Pembroke and his nephew, Henry Tudor, landed in the territories of Duke Francis.  He gave them refuge for ten years and used them skilfully to balance his relationships with England and with France.  Francis lent Henry the money for the unsuccessful invasion of England in 1483.

**François I, King of France, 12 September 1494 – 31 March 1547**
François, King from 1515, was Henry VIII's rival for personal glory, but spent the majority of his life in warfare with Emperor Charles V.  This rivalry prevented France and Spain combining to force Henry VIII back into papal obedience.

**François of Lorraine, d 24 February 1525**   One of the French commanders at the Battle of Pavia at which Richard de la Pole was killed.

**Frulovisi, Tito Livio.**   An Italian scholar employed by Humphrey, Duke of Gloucester, he wrote a memoir of Henry V entitled *Vita Henrici Quinti.*

# G

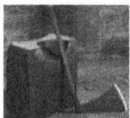

**Galeazzo Maria Sforza, Duke of Milan, 24 January 1444 – 26 December 1476**   A notoriously cruel and sadistic ruler, although a great patron of music, his ambassador at the court of Louis XI, di Bettini, kept the Duke informed of events in England.  His flagrant abuse of power led to his assassination.

**George of York, Duke of Bedford, March 1477 – March 1479**
The third son of Edward IV and Elizabeth Woodville, he died young.

**George, Duke of Clarence, 21 October 1449 – 18 February 1478** The third surviving son of Richard, Duke of York and his Duchess, Cecily Neville, George was created Duke of Clarence when his brother Edward IV took the throne in 1461. Despite the vast lands and wealth with which his brother endowed him, Clarence remained perennially unsatisfied and plotted, first to marry Isabel Neville, daughter of his cousin the Earl of Warwick, against the King's wishes, and then to replace his brother as king. In June 1469 Edward IV marched to capture Clarence and Warwick who escaped to Calais where Clarence married Isabel. On their return, Edward's army was defeated at the Battle of Edgcote and the King was captured by Warwick's men. Warwick was unable to retain control of the country and was forced to free King Edward. Clarence was pardoned but following further insurrection, was obliged to flee to France.

In negotiation between Warwick and Margaret of Anjou, it was agreed that should Edward of Lancaster and his new wife, Warwick's other daughter, have no children, Clarence would be recognised as heir. Henry VI was reinstated by Warwick but Clarence soon realised that he had very little chance of becoming King, and when Edward IV returned with his own army from Burgundy, Clarence threw himself upon his brother's mercy. He was, at least, on the surface, forgiven and reinstated. Clarence fought for his brother at Tewkesbury and, together with the Duke of Gloucester, is alleged to have killed his brother-in-law, Edward of Lancaster, after the battle. Clarence continued to make difficulties in his brother's kingdom and eventually, having lost all patience, Edward brought him before Parliament, where he was tried and convicted of treason. His lands and goods were forfeit and he was executed in the Tower of London, allegedly drowned in a butt of malmsey wine.

**Gough, Matthew. d. 6 July 1450** Leader of a military force, with Lord Scales, raised to defend London against Jack Cade's rebels. Gough was killed during the fighting.

**Gordon, Lady Katherine, c. 1474 – c. 1537** Katharine was the daughter of George Gordon, 2nd Earl of Huntly and a distant cousin of King James IV. She was given as a bride to Perkin Warbeck as part of James's efforts to cause trouble for his southern neighbour, Henry VII. She was well treated at the court of Henry VII, after Warbeck's capture, and continue to live in England until her death.

**Glyndwr, Owain, c. 1349 – c. 1415** Glyndwr, a descendant of the native princes of Wales, led a major rebellion against Henry IV, in which he was supported by the Percys and Mortimers.

**Grafton, Richard d. 1573** Grafton, the King's Printer, published Hall's Chronicles in 1550, the source of much of our knowledge of the period of the Wars of the Roses and the reigns of Henry VII and Henry VIII.

**Grey, Edmund, 4th Baron Grey of Ruthin, 26 October 1416 – 22 May 1490** In his youth, Grey served in France and was a member of the Council of Henry VI. At the Battle of Northampton, he brought his men initially to the Lancastrian side, and was set on the right flank. During the battle he changed sides and took his men into the Yorkist ranks. This devastated the Lancastrians, and they were defeated, with Henry VI being captured. Grey was created Earl of Kent and his two sons were married to sisters of Queen Elizabeth Woodville, Joan and Anne.

**Grey, Edward, first Viscount Lisle, d. 14 October 1492** The son of 3rd Lord Grey of Ruthin, Edward Grey married Elizabeth Talbot, 3rd Baroness Lisle, and was created 1st Viscount Lisle on 28 June 1483. He was summoned by Richard III to join the King at Bosworth.

**Grey, Sir John, of Groby, 1432 – 17 February 1461** The first husband of Elizabeth Woodville, he was killed at the second Battle of St Albans, fighting for Lancaster.

**Grey, Sir Richard, 1457 – 25 June 1483** The second son of Elizabeth Woodville by her first marriage to Sir John Grey of Groby, Richard entered the service of his half-brother, Edward, Prince of Wales, in around 1474. When Edward became King in April 1483, he travelled with him towards London, but the party was intercepted at Stony Stratford by Richard, Duke of Gloucester. Sir Richard was arrested, along with his uncle, Anthony Woodville, Earl Rivers. He was executed without trial on 25 June 1483.

**Grey, Sir Thomas, 1st Marquess of Dorset, c. 1455 – 20 September 1501** Grey was the eldest son of Elizabeth Woodville by her first husband Sir John Grey of Groby. He had a very good relationship with his stepfather, Edward IV. In October 1466, he was married to the King's niece, Anne Holland, daughter of the Lancastrian Duke of Exeter. Anne died young, and Grey then married Cecily Bonville, Baroness Harington, the richest woman in England and niece of the Earl of Warwick. Grey was present at the Battle of Tewkesbury, fighting for Edward IV. Grey was given the title of Marquess of Dorset in 1475. When Edward V became King in April 1483, Grey hoped that he would retain a leading role in any Regency government. This plan was scotched by the usurpation of Richard III. Grey joined the Duke of Buckingham's rebellion and when it failed, escaped to Brittany where he joined Henry Tudor. He decided to leave Henry in early 1485 and returned to England. He was captured and held in France and thus took no part in the Battle of Bosworth. When Henry became King and married Grey's niece, Elizabeth of York, Grey was partially restored to favour, but was never truly trusted by Henry.

# H

**Hall, Edward c. 1498 - 1547** Author of *The Union of the Two Noble and Illustrate Famelies of Lancaster and Yorke*, otherwise known as *Hall's Chronicle*. The Chronicle is a major source of information about the Wars of the Roses and Henry VIII's reign.

**Halle, Jean de**   Leader of a band of marauding criminals, who terrorised Normandy during the anarchic period following the death of Henry V.

**Harcourt, John**  A retainer of William, Lord Hastings, he joined Henry Tudor in exile in Brittany.

**Harris, John**  In 1449 as Henry VI passed through the town of Stony Stratford, en route to a Parliament in Leicester, Harris caused a scene when he waved around an agricultural implement and cried out that the Duke of York would fight in a similar fashion with traitors at the Parliament.  Harris was hanged, drawn and quartered.

**Hastings, William, 1st Baron Hastings, c. 1431 – 13 June 1483** Hastings was a close friend of Edward IV. He fought at the Battle of Mortimer's Cross, a Yorkist victory, and at Towton, which resulted in Edward IV's capturing of the throne. He was nominated as Lord Chamberlain, and was also Master of the Mint.  He and Edward were notorious for their womanising.  Hastings married Lady Katherine Neville, sister of the Earl of Warwick, but remained loyal to Edward IV during the readeption of Henry VI, joining Edward in exile and then returning with him in 1471.  Hasting's stepdaughter, Cecily Bonville, was married to Edward IV's stepson, Thomas, Marquess of Dorset, and Hastings and Dorset were locked in conflict over the heiress's estates. On Edward IV's death, Hastings initially supported Richard, Duke of Gloucester's, plans to make himself Protector as Hastings did not wish Dorset to gain more political power. On 13 June 1483 at a Council meeting in the Tower of London, Richard leapt to his feet, accused Hastings of conspiring against him, had him bundled into the yard and summarily executed.

**Henry IV (of Bolingbroke), King of England, 3 April 1367 – 20 March 1413**  Henry was the oldest son of John of Gaunt, Duke of Lancaster, and first cousin to Richard II. He was exiled for ten years, following a quarrel with Thomas Mowbray, Duke of Norfolk. On Gaunt's death, Richard decided to confiscate the Duchy of Lancaster. Henry invaded, claiming he sought only to have his Duchy restored. However, before long, he had forced Richard II to abdicate. Henry's reign was uneasy – there were numerous supporters of Richard's designated heir, the Earl of March, and uprisings in Wales and the North. Nevertheless he held onto his throne and passed it to his son Henry V.

**Henry V, King of England, 9 August 1387 – 31 August 1422**  On succeeding to the throne in 1413, Henry immediately began planning his invasion and conquest of France. By 1422 he had the divided French realm at his mercy. At the Treaty of Troyes in 1420, it was agreed that Henry would marry Catherine, daughter of Charles VI, and that he would inherit the throne on Charles's death. As it happened, Henry, although much younger than Charles, died first. His own son was only nine months old. Henry left detailed instructions as to how England would be governed and France controlled during the minority of the new King. Such was the force of his personality, and the loyalty of his brothers, that his orders were largely followed.

**Henry VI, King of England, 6 December 1421 – 21 May 1471**  Henry became king at the age of nine months.

During his youth, his realm of England was governed reasonably successfully by a Regency Council. His French possessions were equally well-managed by his uncle, John of Lancaster, Duke of Bedford. Unfortunately, as the King entered his teens, it became apparent that he did not have the force of personality or firmness of character to make him a successful King. In fact he was so indecisive and malleable as to give rise to the suggestion that he was, in fact, mentally deficient and he had a long period of catatonic stupor during the period 1453 to 1454. Although he had been crowned King of France, the English government had neither the money, the manpower nor the talented leaders to maintain this claim. Eventually, amid much recrimination, Henry accepted Charles VII as King of France and agreed to marry his niece. This agreement, brokered by the Duke of Suffolk, was hugely unpopular.

Henry was unable to control the quarrelling amongst the various factions at his court. In particular, his cousin, and next male heir, Richard, Duke of York, believed that Henry's government, first under Suffolk, and then under the Duke of Somerset, was incompetent.

Eventually the rivalry between York and Somerset, supported by Henry's wife, Margaret, broke out into civil war. Henry was never more than the nominal leader of the Lancastrians, who were held together by the vigorous personality of Margaret. Following the Battle of Northampton in 1460, Henry was captured by the Yorkists. He was reunited with his wife following the Battle of Wakefield, but once the Lancastrians were routed at Towton, he was forced into hiding until captured by the Yorkist in 1465 and imprisoned in the Tower of London. Henry was briefly restored as King, a period known as the 'readeption', in 1470 – 71, but was then returned to the Tower as a prisoner following the Yorkist victory at the Battle of Barnet. His son and heir, Edward of Lancaster, Prince of Wales, was killed at Tewkesbury, and Henry VI's body was brought from the Tower a few days later, where, it was said he had died of *'pure displeasure and melancholy'*. There was little doubt in any minds that he had been dispatched on the orders of Edward IV and this is certainly Jones' interpretation.

**Henry VII, King of England, 28 January 1454 – 21 April 1509**
Henry VII was the grandson of Catherine de Valois, Queen of England, by her second marriage to Owen Tudor. His mother, Lady Margaret Beaufort, Countess of Richmond, was a descendant of John of Gaunt, Duke of Lancaster. When Henry was about six years old he was given into the custody of Sir William Herbert, the Yorkist Earl of Pembroke. He was brought up to the age of 14 in Pembroke's household but following the Battle of Edgecote was reunited with his uncle, Jasper Tudor, Earl of Pembroke. When Henry VI was deposed a second time, Henry went into exile in Brittany. In his absence his mother tried to arrange reconciliation with Edward IV. On Edward IV's death, sufficient numbers of Yorkists were so disaffected by the usurpation of Richard III that they were willing to join Henry in exile and to support him in his bid for the throne. Surprisingly given that his claim to the throne was slim and he was little known in England, Henry raised sufficient forces to defeat Richard III at the Battle of Bosworth. He fought off two subsequent attempts to reinstate the House of York, at the Battle of Stoke in 1487 and in various skirmishes led by supporters of Perkin Warbeck. Henry married Elizabeth of York, daughter of Edward IV, and made concerted efforts to reconcile the two parties. The first 16 years of his reign were largely successful, but after the death of his beloved wife and older son in 1503, he retreated into a depressed and avaricious tyranny.

**Henry VIII, King of England, 1491 – 1547** Henry, an extremely accomplished and intelligent man, began his reign in traditional fashion, promoting war with France and expressing strong support for Papal authority. By the late 1520s however, a combination of dynastic fears (he had only one legitimate child, a daughter) and his passion for Anne

Boleyn, led him to request Pope Clement VII to grant an annulment of his marriage. The political situation in Europe did not permit the Pope to accede to this request and Henry sought other alternatives. The advisors and friends of the first twenty years of his reign, Queen Katherine, Cardinal Wolsey, Sir Thomas More, Bishop Fisher, Nicholas Carew and Archbishop Warham, were overthrown in favour of a new group of advisers who could deliver the King's desire.

Henry broke with Rome, took the title Supreme Head of the Church in England and pursued a policy of ruthless repression of all dissent. By 1539, the court had divided into factions, largely based on the religious divide. Henry married a total of six times, but still left a minor heir, a disputed succession, and a country that was almost bankrupt despite the huge injection of cash from the Dissolution of the Monasteries.

 **Herbert, William, 1st Earl of Pembroke, c 1423 – 27 July 1469** The Herberts were rivals for influence in South Wales with Edmund and Jasper Tudor, half-brothers of Henry VI. Herbert was a client of the Duke of York, and, following the Battle of Towton, at which he fought for Edward of York, was granted a barony and the wardship of Jasper Tudor's nephew, Henry. In 1468, Herbert captured Harlech Castle, which had been holding out for Lancaster since the beginning of the Wars. For this triumph he was created Earl of Pembroke and granted the estates of Jasper Tudor, Earl of Pembroke. Herbert's oldest son was married to Mary, sister of Queen Elizabeth Woodville. Herbert fought for Edward IV against Warwick's men at the Battle of Edgecote in 1469. This was a victory for Warwick and the following day Herbert and other Yorkist Lords were executed.

 **Herbert, Sir Richard d. 27 July 1469** The brother of William Herbert, Earl of Pembroke, like his brother he

fought for Edward IV at the Battle of Edgecote, was captured and executed the next day by the Earl of Warwick.

**Holinshed, Raphael c. 1529 – 1580** Holinshed's *Chronicles of England, Scotland and Ireland* were a major source for Shakespeare's interpretation of the Wars of the Roses.

**Holland, Lady Anne, c 1455 – 1474** The daughter of Henry Holland, 3rd Duke of Exeter and his wife, Anne of York, sister of Edward IV, Anne was her father's heiress. She was married, aged 14, to Thomas Grey, Marquess of Dorset, Edward IV's oldest stepson. By a special remainder, Anne's lands were inherited by the daughter of her mother's second marriage, Anne St Leger.

**Holland, John, Earl of Huntingdon, and 2nd Duke of Exeter, 18 March 1395 – 5 August 1447** The son of Elizabeth of Lancaster, and therefore first cousin to Henry V, he was promoted to the dukedom of Exeter, which had been forfeited by his father in 1444.

**Holland, Henry, 3rd Duke of Exeter, 27 June 1430 – September 1475** A minor on the death of his father, his wardship was granted to Richard, Duke of York, who was the father of his wife, Anne of York. Nevertheless, Exeter remained faithful to his second cousin, Henry VI. This attitude may possibly have been encouraged by the fact that during York's Protectorate, Exeter had been imprisoned in Pontefract Castle for disobeying orders to refrain from involvement in the struggles between the Percys and the Nevilles. He was released by Somerset when York's Protectorate ended. He commanded Lancastrian forces at the Battle of Towton, where he was roundly defeated. Exeter joined Queen Margaret in exile in Scotland, and later in France. He was attainted and his lands granted to his wife, Anne of York, before their marriage was annulled in 1472. On the readeption of Henry VI he regained some of his lands and led the Lancastrians at the Battle of Barnet. Badly wounded he was presumed dead but recovered and was reconciled to Edward IV. He served in Edward IV's campaign to France in 1475 but fell overboard from the ship on which he was returning to England, possibly helped on his way.

**Howard, Sir John, 1st Duke of Norfolk, c. 1425 – 22 August 1485** Howard was a supporter of the House of York from the beginning of the Wars of the Roses, and had fought at the Battle of Towton, where he was knighted. He became one of Richard, Duke of Gloucester's closest allies. When Richard became King, Howard was granted the dukedom of Norfolk, previously held by Richard of Shrewsbury, Duke of York when the boy was married to Anne Mowbray, Countess of Norfolk. Howard was the first cousin of Anne's grandfather, the 3rd Duke of Norfolk. Norfolk was one of Richard's most valiant supporters at the Battle of Bosworth, where he was killed. He took no heed of the warning that was allegedly pinned to his tent, reading *'Jock of Norfolk, be not too bold, for Dickon thy master, is bought and sold.'*

**Howard, Thomas, 2nd Duke of Norfolk c. 1448 – 1524** As Earl of Surrey, Howard fought alongside his father, John Howard, 1st Duke of Norfolk, for Richard III at the Battle of Bosworth. Following the battle, he was imprisoned in the Tower of London, but was soon restored to royal favour and appointed as Henry VII's Lieutenant in the North. He served Henry VII valiantly, and transferred his loyalty to Henry VIII. It is owing to Surrey's brilliant generalship, that the English army defeated the superior forces of James IV of Scotland at the Battle of Flodden in 1513. The dukedom of Norfolk was restored in recognition of his services. Howard's granddaughters were Anne Boleyn and Catherine Howard, second and fifth wives of Henry VIII.

**Howard, Catherine, Queen of England, c. 1521 – 13 February 1542** Catherine was the fifth wife of Henry VIII, until she was executed for alleged adultery. During 1541, her tailor had been ordered to make warm clothes for Lady Margaret Pole, Countess of Salisbury who was imprisoned in the Tower. Immediately before her execution, Lady Salisbury prayed for the souls of King Henry, Queen Catherine and Prince Edward.

**Humphrey of Lancaster, Duke of Gloucester, 3 October 1390 – 23 February 1447** The younger brother of Henry V, Gloucester was one of the members of the Regency Council, set up to rule for his baby nephew, Henry VI. Gloucester's interpretation of Henry V's will was that he should personally be Lord Protector, however the other Lords, led by his older brother, John of Lancaster, Duke of Bedford, preferred the conciliar arrangement. He was granted the title of Protector, but only in the absence of Bedford. All ran smoothly enough until Gloucester fell out with his half uncle, Cardinal Henry Beaufort, Bishop of Winchester in 1425. Gloucester was a leader of the War Party which wanted to continue England's military ventures in France, whilst Beaufort sought peace, presumably on the basis that England was financially unable to continue domination of a country far larger and wealthier than itself. Gloucester's and Beaufort's men came to blows in London in 1425. Calm was restored by the other Lords but resentment remained.

Gloucester continued to strive for greater personal power but neither the King's Council nor Parliament would grant it. On the death of the Duke of Bedford, in 1435, Gloucester became heir to the throne. However in 1441 he became embroiled in scandal when his second wife, Eleanor Cobham, was convicted of attempting to foretell the death of the King by sorcery. Following this disgrace it was difficult for Gloucester to retain his pre-eminence.

In 1445, when peace with France was finally negotiated by the Duke of Suffolk, Gloucester remained implacably opposed. To silence him, Suffolk called a Parliament at Bury St Edmunds and Gloucester was summoned to appear at it. He was arrested but before he could be tried, he was found to be gravely ill. At the time it was believed that he had been poisoned although it is certainly possible that he suffered from a stroke, as he lay in a coma for several days before dying. Gloucester's position as leader of the war party, fell upon Richard, Duke of York.

**Hungerford, Sir Walter, 1st Baron Hungerford 22 June 1388 – 1449** Hungerford was appointed as a member of the Regency Council for Henry VI, at an annual salary of £100, and was also one of the men appointed together with Thomas Beaufort, Duke of Exeter, as a guardian of the person of the young King. When Owen Tudor, the widower of Catherine de Valois, was imprisoned for his temerity in marrying the Royal widow, he was guarded by Sir Walter, at Windsor Castle. Hungerford's son and grandson remained loyal Lancastrians.

**Hungerford, Sir Walter, d. 1516** Like his great-grandfather, grandfather and father, Sir Walter was a Lancastrian. Arrested when Richard III became aware that Henry Tudor had landed at Milford Haven, Hungerford escaped and fought for Henry at the Battle of Bosworth. He was a Privy Councillor to both Henry VII and Henry VIII.

# I

**Iden, Alexander, Sheriff of Kent** Iden captured the rebel Jack Cade in 1450.

**Isabeau of Bavaria, Queen of France, 1371 – 28 September 1435** Isabeau was the wife of Charles VI of France and the mother of Catherine de Valois. She had been a supporter of the Burgundians against the

Armagnacs and she was instrumental in agreeing the Treaty of Troyes, whereby her son, Charles VII, would be disinherited in favour of her daughter's husband, Henry V of England. She was present when her grandson, Henry VI of England, was crowned King of France.

**Isabella of Castile, Queen of Castile. 22 April 1451 – 26 November 1504** Isabella was proposed as a wife for Edward IV in the 1460s, prior to his secret marriage to Elizabeth Woodville. Allegedly Isabella was much offended by Edward's rejection of her. Isabella and her husband, Ferdinand of Aragon, recognised Henry VII as King of England in the Treaty of Medina del Campo, in which her daughter Katherine was betrothed to Henry VII's son, Arthur. Apparently Isabella's concerns about the safety of Henry's throne were alleviated when he agreed to the execution of Edward, Earl of Warwick.

**Isabella of France, Queen of England, 1295 – 22 August 1358** Wife of Edward II, Isabella had originally supported her husband, even in the face of his depressing attachment to his male favourites. Eventually, however, offended by the behaviour of the Despensers, she orchestrated the King's overthrow, together with her lover, Roger Mortimer. Isabella was the daughter of Philip IV of France and it was through her that her son Edward III claimed the French throne.

**Isabelle of Lorraine, Duchess of Lorraine and Anjou, Queen of Naples 1400 – 28 February 1453** Isabelle took an active part in the government of her own Duchy, and also as Regent for her husband, René of Anjou. She led an army to rescue René from captivity by the Burgundians. Isabelle, her husband René, and her mother-in-law, Yolanda of Aragon, were all supporters of the Armagnac party in France.

**Isabelle of Valois, Queen of England, 9 November 1389 – 13 September 1409.** Following the death of his beloved wife, Anne of Bohemia, Richard II married the child Isabelle of Valois, whose youth made it unlikely that the King would sire an heir for some time. Isabelle was deeply attached to her husband, and rejected the proposition made by Henry IV, after he deposed Richard, that she should marry his heir, later Henry V. Isabelle returned to France and died young in childbirth. In the event Henry V married her younger sister, Catherine.

## Jacqueline to Oldhall

# J

**Jacqueline of Hainault, Duchess of Gloucester, 1401 – 8 October 1436** Jacqueline was Countess of Hainault, and other territories, in her own right, but was challenged by her male relatives. Her husband John, Duke of Brabant, eventually sold her birthright. She left John, and requested an annulment of her marriage. Forced into exile in England she was well-received by Henry V and was godmother to Henry VI. An annulment was granted in England, and she married Henry V's brother, Humphrey, Duke of Gloucester. The couple remained childless. Gloucester supported his wife's claims, which created difficulties as her opponents were the Burgundian faction allied to England in France. Gloucester abandoned Jacqueline, perhaps from a desire to avoid the political and military situation as well as because he wanted to marry the beautiful Eleanor Cobham. Pope Martin V declared her marriage to Gloucester null and void and Jacqueline was obliged to retire to the small estate she was granted after 'voluntarily' resigning her lands to the Duke of Burgundy.

**Jacquetta of Luxembourg, Duchess of Bedford, c 1415 – 30 May 1472** Jacquetta was married at the age of 17 to John of Lancaster, Duke of Bedford, as part of the Burgundian alliance with England against France. She was widowed within a couple of years, and secretly married Sir Richard Woodville. The marriage was one of great social disparity and created a furore. Nevertheless the Woodvilles went on to have 14 children. Jacquetta retained the rank of her first husband and was an important figure at the Lancastrian court, and lady-in-waiting to Margaret of Anjou. In 1465, however, she seized the opportunity when Edward IV became enamoured of her daughter Elizabeth, the widow of

Sir John Grey of Groby. Jacquetta was present when they married in secret and was godmother their first child, Elizabeth of York. In 1469, she was accused by the Earl of Warwick and the Duke of Clarence of having used sorcery to ensnare the King.

**Jakeman, Agnes** Chamber woman to Henry VI as a baby.

**James I, King of Scots, 25 July 1394 – 21 February 1437** James had been captured at the age of 12 in English waters, and had been held prisoner ever since. He was treated as an honoured guest, but was not allowed to return home to Scotland until he had entered into a treaty with the English under which he married Lady Joan Beaufort, half cousin of Henry V. He was released on return to Scotland in 1424, not necessarily to the delight of his relatives. He was assassinated in 1437.

**James IV of Scotland, 17 March 1473 – 9 September 1513** James IV was one of the European monarchs who supported Perkin Warbeck with money, men and even a wife. Eventually, however, he came to terms with Henry VII, whose daughter Margaret he married in 1503. James was killed at the Battle of Flodden on 9 September 1513, by the forces of his brother-in-law, Henry VIII.

**Jeanne de Bourbon, Queen of France, 23 April 1464 – 4 February 1505** Jeanne was the daughter of Louis XI and sister of Charles VIII. As France did not recognise female inheritance of the Crown, she was married to Louis of Orleans, the next heir. On Charles's death, Jeanne became Queen Consort of France but was swiftly divorced. She was granted the Duchy of Berry and lived in retirement.

**Jean, Count of Dunois, the Bastard of Orleans, 23 November 1402 - 24 November 1468** Dunois was the commander of Joan of Arc's forces, when the French raised the Siege of Orleans on 8 May 1429.

**Joan of Arc, c 1412 - 30 May 1431** A 17-year-old girl from Lorraine, she persuaded the Dauphin Charles to give her troops to relieve the city of Orleans, which had been besieged by the English for over a year. The astonished Dauphin was persuaded by her sincerity, and she was as good as her word. Orleans was relieved and Charles was crowned King of France. A year later Joan was captured by the Burgundians, and sold to the English. She was tried for heresy and burnt in Rouen.

**Joan of Navarre, Queen of England, 1370 – 1437** By her first marriage, Joan was Duchess of Brittany, and acted as Regent for her son, John V. In 1403 she married the widowed Henry IV of England. The couple had no children but she was on good terms with his sons. In 1419 she was accused of witchcraft and imprisoned for four years.

**John the Fearless, Duke of Burgundy, 28 May 1371 – 10 September 1419.** John and his nephew, Louis of Orleans, were locked in conflict over who should be Regent for John's nephew, Charles VI of France. On 23 November 1407, Louis was murdered on John's orders. France degenerated into civil war between the Burgundians and the supporters of Louis' son Charles, the Armagnacs. On 10 September 1419 John was in his turn, murdered.

**John of Gaunt, Duke of Lancaster, 6 March 1340 – 3 February 1399** John was the third son of Edward III. He married three times, first to his cousin Blanche of Lancaster, which brought the Lancastrian estates back into the royal family. He and Blanche had three children who grew up, Henry IV, Philippa of Lancaster, Queen of Portugal, and Elizabeth of Lancaster, Duchess of Exeter. By his second wife, Constance of Castile, John had another daughter, Katherine of Lancaster, Queen of Castile. By his third wife, Katherine Swynford (née de Roet), he had four children, who were all born prior to their marriage. These four children were given the surname Beaufort. His senior male descendants were the Lancastrian kings. Through his oldest Beaufort son he was the ancestor of Henry VII and through his youngest daughter, Joan Beaufort, he was also the ancestor of Edward IV and Richard III.

**John of Lancaster, Duke of Bedford, 20 June 1389 – 14 September 1435** John was the third son of Henry IV, but second only to his brother, Henry V, in military and political skill. On Henry V's death Bedford was appointed to manage the English possessions in France. On 17 August 1424 he achieved a stunning victory at the Battle of Verneuil. Bedford was married to Anne of Burgundy, sister of the English ally, the Duke of Burgundy. He was a successful Governor of Normandy, but following his death in 1435 the English steadily lost control. Bedford, like his brother Gloucester, was a great patron of the arts. His illuminated Book of Hours, housed at the British Library, is one of the treasures of the early 15<sup>th</sup> century.

**John of Pontefract** An illegitimate son of Richard III, he was knighted by his father and appointed as Captain of Calais in 1485. The last certain knowledge of John was the grant to him of the pension of 20 marks per annum by Henry VII on 1 March 1486.

**Joanna I, Queen of Castile, 6 November 1479 – 12 April 1555** Joanna, daughter of Ferdinand of Aragon and Isabella of Castile, was married to Philip the Fair, Duke of Burgundy. She and Philip were shipwrecked in England in 1506 on their way to Spain to claim Joanna's kingdom of Castile. They were treated as honoured guests but no ships could be found to return them to Spain until Philip and his father, the Emperor Maximilian, had agreed to hand over Edmund de la Pole to Henry VII. Joanna spent most of the rest of her life under restraint, allegedly suffering from madness.

# K

**Katherine of Aragon, Queen of England, 16 December 1485 – 6 January 1536** Daughter of Ferdinand of Aragon and Isabella of Castile, Katherine came to England in 1501 to marry Arthur, Prince of Wales in fulfilment of the Treaty of Medina del Campo. On Arthur's death, it was agreed she would marry his brother, Henry, and a dispensation for the marriage was granted by the Pope, allowing for either the consummation or non-consummation of the first marriage. In fact, the match did not take place until Henry succeeded to the throne in 1509. Katherine was exceptionally well educated and intelligent, a patron of learning and a woman who inspired great personal loyalty. She and Henry lived happily together for some sixteen years, although only one child, Mary, survived more than a few weeks.

By 1525, with Katherine past child-bearing, Henry was looking elsewhere for an heir. Simultaneously, he became enamoured of Anne Boleyn. Henry requested the Pope to grant an annulment of his marriage to Katherine, on the basis that the dispensation was not valid, as the Pope could not dispense in the particular case. Katherine argued that as her first marriage had not been consummated, her second marriage was valid. Initially, Henry tried to persuade Katherine by gentle means, but she was adamant that she would not back down. Supported by her powerful nephew, Emperor Charles V, Katherine fought the annulment to the bitter end, refusing to accept the verdict given by Archbishop Cranmer in 1533 that the marriage was invalid, and that she was not Queen, but merely Princess Dowager of Wales. She was sent to increasingly isolated castles and parted from her daughter. She died in 1536, signing herself Katherine the Queen.

**Katherine of York, Countess of Devon, 14 August 1479 – 15 November 1527**  Katherine was the fifth daughter of Edward IV and Queen Elizabeth Woodville.  On her father's death she retreated to sanctuary at Westminster Abbey with her mother, sisters and brother, Richard of Shrewsbury, Duke of York.  When Queen Elizabeth and her daughters were finally persuaded to emerge, the sisters were promised that they would be married honourably.  When her older sister, Elizabeth of York, became Henry VII's Queen, Katherine was a member of her household.  When she was 20 she was married to William Courtenay, Earl of Devon.  Although he came under suspicion of treason and was imprisoned, Katherine herself remained free.  She had two children, Margaret and Henry.  When her nephew, Henry VIII, inherited the throne she was one of the most important court ladies, and stood godmother to his daughter, Mary.

**Kemp, Cardinal John, Archbishop of Canterbury, c. 1380 – 22 March 1454**  Kemp was Chancellor to Henry VI and a loyal servant of the King and Margaret of Anjou.

**Kerver, Thomas**  In 1444 Thomas Kerver, bailiff to the Abbot of Reading, was brought before the King's Bench accused of treason.  The sentence of hanging, drawing and quartering was begun but before it was completed Kerver was cut down and taken away.  Apparently this was upon the orders of the King.  Kerver spent some time in prison before being released.

**Kynaston, Sir Roger of Hordley c. 1433 – 1495**  Kynaston was one of the Duke of York's retainers.  At the Battle of Blore Heath on 23 April 1459, he was involved in the death of Lord Audley, the Lancastrian commander.

**Kyriell, Sir Thomas, 1396 – 1461**  Kyriell was appointed by the Yorkists to guard the captured Henry VI who had been brought to the battlefield of St Albans.  This was a

Lancastrian victory, and Kyriell and his fellow guard, Lord Bonville, were summarily executed on Queen Margaret's orders.

# L

**Landais, Pierre, Treasurer of Brittany, 1430 – 1485** Landais was one of Francis II, Duke of Brittany's, most important advisers. He worked with Francis to use Henry Tudor as a bargaining tool with both England and France. In 1484, during a period of illness on the part of Duke Francis, Richard III agreed with Landais that in return for 4000 soldiers to defend Brittany against the French, Henry Tudor would be handed over. Henry got wind of the plot, and escaped to France with only moments to spare. On his recovery Duke Francis was horrified that his hospitality had been so undermined and committed Henry's other followers to join him at court of France. Landais had numerous enemies and was eventually tortured and executed.

**Lionel of Antwerp, Duke of Clarence, 29 November 1338 – 17 October 1368** The second son of Edward III, Lionel's great-grandson, Edmund Mortimer, Earl of March, was nominated as his successor by Richard II. Edmund's claim passed to his nephew, Richard, Duke of York.

**Louis de Valois, Duke of Orleans, 13 March 1372 – 23 November 1407** Louis attempted to become the Governor of France during the frequent periods of insanity of his brother, Charles VI. This led to murderous conflict with his uncle, John the Fearless, Duke of Burgundy. Louis was murdered in the streets of Paris on his uncle's orders.

**Louis IX, 25 April 1214 – 25 August 1270** Louis IX, later canonised, was one of France's most successful mediaeval Kings. Men who are descended in unbroken male line from Louis were considered to be 'Princes du Sang', and eligible to inherit the throne.

**Louis X, King of France, 4 October 1289 – 5 June 1316**  Louis was the oldest son of Philip IV of France, and the brother of Isabella of France, Queen of England.

**Louis XI, King of France, 3 July 1423 – 30 August 1483**  Louis inherited the throne of France on 22 July 1461.  He granted asylum to Margaret of Anjou, although he did not keep her in any great state.  He gave her some military support in 1463 until in October of that year he entered a peace treaty with Edward IV that prohibited him from aiding the Lancastrians.  It was with Louis XI that Warwick was negotiating for a French alliance to be cemented by the marriage of Edward IV to Louis' sister-in-law, Bona of Savoy. The news that Edward was already married to Elizabeth Woodville, unsurprisingly, brought the negotiations to a crashing halt.  Edward's subsequent alliance with Burgundy, through the marriage of his sister, Margaret of York, to Charles, Duke of Burgundy, drove Louis again into supporting the Lancastrians.  He funded a small invasion by Jasper Tudor, Earl of Pembroke in 1468 and it was Louis who organised a reconciliation between Warwick and Margaret of Anjou which led to the readeption of Henry VI.  After the loss at the Battle of Tewkesbury and the deaths of Henry VI and Edward of Lancaster, Prince of Wales, Louis ransomed Margaret of Anjou in 1475.  It was with Louis XI that Edward IV agreed the Treaty of Picquiny in 1475.  Louis also negotiated a treaty with Burgundy in 1483, which was a blow for England.

**Louis XII, King of France, 27 June 1462 – 1 January 1515**  Louis inherited the throne from his distant cousin, and brother-in-law, Charles VIII, in May 1498.  In retaliation for Henry VIII's invasion of France in 1513, Louis recognised Richard de la Pole as the rightful king of England.  In the treaty which ended Henry's war in France, Louis was married to

Mary, younger daughter of Henry VII, known subsequently as Mary, the French Queen.

**Lovell, John, 8th Baron Lovell, 1433 – 1465** On his death, his son, Francis, being underage, was given by Edward IV into the wardship of Richard Neville, Earl of Warwick.

**Lovell, Francis, 1st Viscount Lovell, 1444 – after 1488** Lovell was a ward of Richard Neville, Earl of Warwick and was brought up with Richard, Duke of Gloucester with whom he enjoyed a long and enduring friendship. When Richard took the throne as Richard's the third, Lovell was one of his closest advisers – as remembered in the rhyme *'the cat, the rat and Lovell the dog rule all England under a hog.'* Lovell was appointed to guard the south coast of England against possible invasion by Henry Tudor. Following the battle of Bosworth he fled into sanctuary and then after a failed rebellion in Yorkshire, escaped to the court of Margaret of York, Dowager Duchess of Burgundy. Lovell was involved in the Lambert Simnel rebellion and fought at the battle of Stoke in 1487. It is uncertain whether Lovell escaped from the battle or not, Jones lists him as amongst the fallen but other sources believe he escaped.

**Lovell, John, 8th Baron Lovell, 1433 – 1465** On his death, his son, Francis, being underage, was given by Edward IV into the wardship of Richard Neville, Earl of Warwick.

**Lovell, Sir Thomas, d. 1524** Lovell joined Henry Tudor in Brittany, after the death of Edward IV. Following the Battle of Bosworth he received a number of positions in the new King's household. He was Speaker of the House of Commons in Henry VII's first Parliament and on 10 December 1485 conveyed Parliament's desire that Henry VII should marry *'that illustrious Lady Elizabeth, daughter of King Edward IV'*. Lovell remained one of Henry's most important advisers and also served under Henry VIII until he retired from public affairs in around 1515.

**Lydgate, John, c. 1370 – c. 1450** A Benedictine monk, Lydgate was a poet, patronised by many of the most educated men at Henry VI's court, in particular Humphrey, Duke of Gloucester, the King's uncle. He wrote and translated copious amounts of poetry, including various works supportive of Henry VI's claim to the French throne.

# M

**Mancini, Dominic** Mancini visited England sometime in the period 1482 to 1483. He wrote a contemporaneous report for his patron, the Archbishop of Vienne, in which he describes the events in England immediately before and after the death of Edward IV. The report came to light in 1934.

**Marie of Anjou, Queen of France, 14 October 1404 – 29 November 1463** Wife of Charles VII of France, and mother of Louis XI of France, as well as 13 other children. Her niece, Margaret, became Queen of England.

**Margaret of Anjou, Queen of England, 23 March 1430 – 25 August 1482** Margaret was the daughter of Duke René of Anjou whose sister, Marie, was the wife of Charles VII of France. In 1444, the Earl (later Duke) of Suffolk, Henry VI's most trusted adviser sought peace with France. It was apparent to all but the most belligerent that England could no longer afford to continue the war. He agreed a truce with Charles of France and peace was to be cemented by the marriage of Margaret to Henry VI. She was married by proxy in the Cathedral of Tours on 24 May 1444, aged just 14. She arrived in England the following April and married Henry in person. Although Henry seems to have immediately become fond of her Margaret did not conceive for several years. During the first years of her marriage, Margaret would have become aware that her husband's nobles were jockeying for control of government. Suffolk, who had arranged her marriage, was impeached and lynched in 1450. Her husband's two cousins Richard, Duke of York and Edmund, Duke of Somerset, were locked in a personal feud. Margaret clearly favoured Somerset and, coming from a background of factional politics in France, did not seem able to lift the Crown above faction. In 1453, when Henry VI fell into a catatonic state, York was proclaimed as Protector. During that year Margaret bore her only child, Edward of Lancaster, Prince of Wales. As soon as Henry recovered, Margaret brought Somerset back to the forefront of politics. By 1455, civil war was clearly brewing.

Throughout the years 1455 to 1461, Margaret was the strength behind the Lancastrians' efforts to keep control of the kingdom. Following the Battle of Towton in 1461, Edward, son of Richard, Duke of York claimed the throne as Edward IV. Margaret fought a rearguard action, from her exile in Scotland and France. In 1469, she was apparently reconciled with Richard Neville Earl of Warwick, who had once been her bitterest enemy. Warwick invaded England, drove Edward IV into exile and released Henry VI from the Tower of London. Unfortunately by the time Margaret arrived, with another Lancastrian army, Edward IV had returned from Burgundy, and defeated Warwick at the Battle of Barnet. Margaret and her son raced to meet up with the Lancastrians under Jasper Tudor, but were defeated in a final terrible battle at Tewkesbury. Her son and husband both dead, Margaret spent several years imprisoned before being released to her cousin Louis XI of France. In Jones' largely sympathetic interpretation of Margaret's character, he emphasises the strong female role models that she had had in childhood: her aunt, the Queen of France, her mother, Isabelle, sovereign Duchess of Lorraine, and her grandmother, Yolanda of Aragon, who was one of the most powerful women in France.

**Margaret, Princess of Scotland, c 1455 – unknown** Daughter of James II of Scotland, Margaret was proposed as a wife for a number of Englishmen: Edward of Lancaster, Prince of Wales; George, Duke of Clarence and Anthony Woodville, Earl Rivers. In the event she married none of them and was disgraced for becoming the mistress, perhaps not entirely voluntarily, of Lord Crichton, by whom she had a daughter.

**Margaret, Queen of Scots, 28 November 1489 – 18 October 1541** The eldest daughter of Henry VII and Elizabeth of York, Margaret was married to James IV of Scotland to seal the Treaty of Perpetual Peace in 1503. Margaret's descendants have reigned in both England and Scotland since 1603.

**Margaret of York, Duchess of Burgundy, 3 May 1446 – 23 November 1503** Margaret was the devoted sister of Edward IV and Richard III. In July 1468, she was married to Charles the Bold, Duke of Burgundy, as his third wife. She had no children but was on good terms with her stepdaughter, Mary. Margaret's marriage to Burgundy was one of the factors which led Louis XI to support the Lancastrian invasion of 1469. Following this invasion, Edward IV escaped to Burgundy where he threw himself on the mercy of Margaret's husband. Initially, Charles had little inclination to support him but eventually he decided that England under Edward IV was preferable to Lancastrian England, allied to Louis XI. Following Charles's death in 1477, Margaret gave support and guidance to the new Duchess and was on good terms with Mary's husband, Maximilian, King of the Romans. Once Henry VII took the Crown, Margaret was an inveterate supporter of Yorkist plots, in particular she claimed to recognise Perkin Warbeck as her nephew and gave him unstinting support.

**Martin V, Pope, 1369 – 20 February 1431** Martin V created Henry Beaufort, Bishop of Winchester, Cardinal in 1417, with an additional responsibility to stamp out heresy in the Hussite stronghold of Hungary.

The Pope refused to recognise the Treaty of Troyes, which undermined England's claim to be the legitimate inheritors of the Crown, following the death of Charles VI.

**Mary I, Queen of England, 18 February 1516 – 17 November 1558** The daughter of Henry VIII and Katherine of Aragon, she was her father's pampered darling until she sided with her mother over the annulment. During the period 1525 – 8 she was treated as Princess of Wales (although never given the title) and looked likely to be accepted as Henry's heir. However, when Henry made the decision to seek an annulment of his marriage to Katherine to marry Anne Boleyn, Mary lost her place. Separated from her mother in 1531, she was sent away from Court, and, in 1533 had her household disbanded whilst she was sent to act as Lady-in-Waiting to Anne's daughter, Elizabeth. On Anne's death in 1536, Mary appealed to Cromwell for him to intercede with her father for her. In an increasingly severe series of letters, Cromwell, presumably with Henry's knowledge, bullied Mary into signing the Acts of Supremacy and Succession. Once this was done, Mary was re-united with her father, and became a close friend of his new wife, Jane Seymour. Mary was a prominent figure at her father's court for most of the rest of his reign. Eventually restored to the succession in her father's will, she fought off an attempt to deprive her of the Crown on the death of Edward VI. As England's first female monarch, Mary had a difficult path to follow, and her short reign is remembered as disastrous (although the facts are more nuanced).

**Mary, Duchess of Burgundy, 13 February 1457 – 27 March 1482** Mary was the greatest heiress in Europe and her hand was fought over by numerous suitors. George, Duke of Clarence was one possible contender, but this plan was blocked by his brother, Edward IV. The eventual winner was Maximilian of Habsburg, King of the Romans. Mary died at the age of 25, following a riding accident, and her lands passed to her son, Philip the Fair, Duke of Burgundy.

**Mary of Guelders, 1434 – 1 December 1463**  The widow of James II of Scotland and Regent for her son, James III, Mary was considered as a possible wife for Edward IV.

**Mary, the French Queen, 18 March 1496 – 25 June 1533**  Mary was the second daughter of Henry VII and Elizabeth of York.  She was betrothed at the age of 11 to Charles of Castile, later the Emperor Charles V.  Charles and his grandfather, the Emperor Maximilian, dragged their feet over completing the marriage and Henry VIII took the opportunity to marry his sister to the aged Louis XII of France.  After brief period as Queen of France, Mary returned to England having secretly married her brother's friend, Charles Brandon, Duke of Suffolk by whom she was the grandmother of Lady Jane Grey.

**Mary of York, 1467 – 1482**  The second child of Edward IV and Elizabeth Woodville, Mary died at the age of about 15.

**Marillac, Charles de, c. 1510 – 2 December 1560**  Ambassador of François I to England during the 1540s.  He reported on Henry VIII's marriage to Anne of Cleves, and also on the death of Lady Margaret Pole (Plantagenet), Countess of Salisbury.

**Maychell, John.**  A Cumbrian farmer, he gave refuge to Henry VI during 1464 when the former king secretly returned to England.

**Meno, Pregent**  Meno was a Breton merchant who employed a young man by the name of Pierrechon Warbecq, commonly known as Perkin Warbeck.  Meno landed in court in Dublin in late 1491, and his assistant was immediately seized upon as a tool which the Yorkists could use to unseat Henry VII.

**Merfeld, John and William** In 1450 these two brothers were brought before the court for claiming that Henry VI was simple-minded and ought to be replaced as King.

**Mitton, Thomas, Bailiff of Shrewsbury** On 17 August 1485, Mitton lowered the portcullis on the western gate of Shrewsbury, to prevent the entrance of Henry Tudor and his army. Mitton claimed that he would only permit Henry to pass *'over his belly'*. On receiving a message from the Stanley brothers, the most important Lords in the region, Mitton opened the gates, lay down in the road and permitted Henry to pass over him.

**Moleyns, Adam, Bishop of Chichester d. 9 January 1450** An ally of the Duke of Suffolk and Queen Margaret of Anjou, Moleyns was Lord Privy Seal. For reasons that are not fully known, but that may have been political or personal in motive, he was murdered in Plymouth en route to the Holy Land.

**Montacute, Thomas, 4th Earl of Salisbury, 13 June 1388 – 3 November 1428** One of the English leaders at the victory of Verneuil, he was killed during the Siege of Orleans. His daughter Alice, married to Richard Neville, brother of Cecily Neville, Duchess of York, inherited the earldom.

**Mortimer, Sir Edmund, 10 December 1376 – 1409.** Mortimer took part in the revolt of Owain Glyndwr, and supported the claim of his nephew, Edmund Mortimer, 4th Earl of March, to be the rightful king, rather than Henry IV.

**Mortimer, Sir Roger, 1st Earl of March, 25 April 1287 – 29 November 1330** Mortimer was the lover of Isabella of France, Queen of England. Together they deposed her unsatisfactory husband, Edward II, initially with significant public support, but when they showed themselves to be little better than

Edward II, they rapidly lost popularity. When Isabella's son, Edward III, was 17, he asserted his own authority and Mortimer was hanged.

**Morton, John, Bishop of Ely, c. 1420 – 1500(Later Cardinal and Archbishop of Canterbury)** Morton was a member of Edward IV's Council. He was involved in the Duke of Buckingham's rebellion, and was attainted by Parliament. Morton's support for Henry Tudor was an important factor in the latter's successful bid for the throne. Under Henry VII he became Archbishop of Canterbury, and Lord Chancellor.

**Morton, Robert, Master of the Rolls. 1435 – May 1497** Morton, nephew of the Bishop of Ely, was Master of the Rolls from 1479. On 22 September 1483, he was relieved of his position by Richard III who suspected that Morton and his uncle were involved in plots against him. Under Henry VII he became Bishop of Worcester.

**Mowbray, Anne, Countess and Duchess of Norfolk, Duchess of York, 10 December 1472 – 1481** Anne was the only living child of John Mowbray, 4th Duke of Norfolk. The earldom of Norfolk was heritable in the female line, and Anne became 8th Countess. In order to secure this rich inheritance for one of his sons, Edward IV arranged the marriage of Anne to his younger son, Richard of Shrewsbury, Duke of York. The dukedom of Norfolk was then bestowed on Richard and, contrary to normal practice, he and his heirs were granted the reversion of Anne's estates.

**Mowbray, John, 3rd Duke of Norfolk, 12 September 1415 – 6 November 1461** A friend and associate of Richard, Duke of York during the 1440s, he was reluctant to commit himself to armed support until the Battle of Northampton in 1460 at which he fought for the Yorkists. He also supported them at the second Battle of St Albans on 17 February 1461. He supported Edward in his claim to be King in early 1461 and played an important part in the Battle of Towton.

**Mowbray, John 4th Duke of Norfolk, 18 October 1440 – 14 January 1476** Norfolk attended the coronation of Elizabeth Woodville. On his death his earldom of Norfolk passed to his daughter, Anne.

**Mowbray, Sir Thomas de 1st Duke of Norfolk, 22 March 1368 – 22 September 1399** Mowbray was one of the Lords Appellant, who sought to control the tyranny of Richard II. He was banished from England by Richard, following a quarrel with Henry Bolingbroke, later Henry IV.

# N

**Neville, Anne, Duchess of Buckingham, 1414 – 20 September 1480** Anne Neville was the sister of Richard Neville, Earl of Salisbury, and Cecily Neville, Duchess of York. Anne was married in around 1424 to Humphrey Stafford, 1st Duke of Buckingham, by whom she had five children, including Sir Henry Stafford who married the widowed Lady Margaret Beaufort, Countess of Richmond in 1455. Buckingham was a Lancastrian and their eldest son, another Humphrey, was killed fighting for Lancaster at the first Battle of St Albans. In 1459, after the defeat of the Yorkists at Ludford Bridge, Anne's sister, Cecily, and her younger children were put into her care. Buckingham was killed at the Battle of Northampton. Anne's second son, Sir Henry Stafford, was reconciled to Edward IV after fighting for Lancaster at the Battle of Towton, but died of wounds sustained at Barnet. Anne's grandson, Henry, 2nd Duke of Buckingham, although a supporter of Edward IV, rebelled against Richard III. Anne married a second time to Walter Blount, Lord Mountjoy. She outlived all but one of her children.

**Neville, Anne, Queen of England 11 June 1456 – 9 March 1485** Anne was the younger of the two daughters of Richard Neville, Earl of Warwick. In 1469, aged 13, she was taken by her parents to France, following Warwick's decision to undo the work of his whole life and restore Henry VI to the throne. It was agreed that Anne would marry Edward of Lancaster, Prince of Wales. She remained in France with her mother, her new husband and her mother-in-law, Margaret of Anjou, whilst Warwick headed an invasion. In early 1471 the little Lancastrian Royal family returned to England, to the dreadful news that Warwick had been killed at the Battle of Barnet. The group, together with their army, headed for Tewkesbury, to meet Lancastrian reinforcements. On 4 April 1471 at the Battle of Tewkesbury, Anne's husband was killed, either during the battle or immediately thereafter. With the Lancastrian cause apparently dead, Anne and the other women were taken to London. Anne was put into the care of her sister, Isabel, Duchess of Clarence. For reasons that are not known, Anne left Clarence's house and disguised herself as a kitchen maid. This may have been because she wished to marry Richard, Duke of Gloucester and Clarence forced her into hiding to prevent it, or because she did not wish to marry the Duke and was hoping to hide from him. Regardless, in 1472 she married Richard, by whom she had one son, Edward of Middleham. For the next nine years Anne lived largely in the North of England. When Richard took the throne in 1483 she was crowned beside him at Westminster Abbe y. She lost her son the following April, and she herself died in March 1485, possibly of tuberculosis.

**Neville, Cecily, Duchess of York, 3 May 1415 – 31 May 1495**
Cecily was the youngest child of Ralph Neville, 1st Earl of Westmorland and Joan Beaufort, daughter of John of Gaunt, Duke of Lancaster. She was married at the age of 14 to her father's ward, Richard, Duke of York. During the 1430s and 1440s Cecily accompanied her husband and his various missions in France and Ireland, during which period she bore some 11 children. She was on better terms with Margaret of Anjou than was her husband but there was never any question as to her loyalties. Following the Battle of Ludford Bridge after which her husband and

oldest two sons fled abroad, Cecily and her younger children were confined in the care of her sister, Anne, Duchess of Buckingham. She was briefly reunited with York following the Battle of Northampton but widowed in December 1460, following the Battle of Wakefield. On the accession of her son as Edward IV, Cecily, known as My Lady the King's Mother, was a prominent figure at court. It is alleged that she disliked her daughter-in-law Elizabeth Woodville. When Henry VII became King, and her granddaughter Queen, Cecily lived largely in retirement, devoting herself to religious causes.

**Neville, George, Bishop of Exeter, Lord Chancellor, 1432 – 8 June 1476** Son of Richard Neville, Earl of Salisbury, Neville was a firm supporter of York. When his cousin, Edward of York, claimed the throne in 1460 Neville gave a speech to the citizens of London outlining Edward's claim and rallying their support. In Edward's government he was given the role of Lord Chancellor, and later Archbishop of York. Neville's primary loyalty was to his brother, Richard Neville, Earl of Warwick, and when Warwick rebelled against Edward IV, Neville supported him. He was pardoned for this but at a later time was accused of treason and held prisoner for two years at Hammes Castle near Calais.

 **Neville, Sir Henry, d. 26 July 1469** Neville, a cousin of Richard, Earl of Warwick and of Edward IV, supported Warwick in his rebellion against the King. He died at the Battle of Edgecote.

**Neville, Isabel, Duchess of Clarence, 5 September 1451 – 12 December 1476** The eldest daughter of Richard, Earl of Warwick, she was married to George, Duke of Clarence, brother of Edward IV, and at that time the King's heir, in defiance of the King's express orders. Although the earldom of Warwick was actually her mother's, the King permitted Clarence and his brother Gloucester, who was married to Isabel's sister, Anne, to divide the lands of the earldom between them as though the Countess were 'naturally dead'. Isabel bore two children, Margaret, and Edward, Earl of Warwick, before dying young in childbed. The execution of Isabel's daughter is seen by Jones as the final close of the Wars of the Roses.

**Neville, Katherine, Duchess of Norfolk, circa 1401 – after 1483**
The second of the numerous children of Ralph Neville, first Earl of Westmorland and his wife Joan Beaufort, Katherine was the sister of Cecily, Duchess of York, Anne, Duchess of Buckingham, Richard, Earl of Salisbury, and Eleanor, Duchess of Northumberland. Katherine had four husbands: John, 2nd Duke of Norfolk by whom she had John, 3rd Duke of Norfolk, a Yorkist; Thomas Strangeways; John, Viscount Beaumont, who died for Lancaster at the Battle of Northampton and finally, in a grotesque match that shocked the court, John Woodville, brother of Queen Elizabeth Woodville and some 45 years her junior, whom she outlived.

**Neville, John, Marquess of Montague c. 1431 – 14 April 1471** Son of the Earl of Salisbury, Neville fought at Blore Heath for York but was captured on his return and imprisoned in Chester Castle. In 1461 he was present together with Warwick at the second Battle of St Albans, a Yorkist victory. When his cousin, Edward IV, became King, Neville shared in the spoils, first receiving the title of Montague and then the forfeited Percy title of Earl of Northumberland. He repaid his cousin with his loyalty when Warwick first rebelled but Neville was disappointed when Northumberland was returned to Percy. He received new lands and a marquessate but when Warwick reinstated Henry VI, Neville joined his brother, being killed with him at the Battle of Barnet.

**Neville, Richard, Earl of Salisbury, 1430 - December 1460** The oldest son of Ralph Neville, 1st Earl of Westmorland by his second wife, Joan Beaufort, daughter of

John of Gaunt Duke of Lancaster, Salisbury was a devoted friend and follower of his brother-in-law, Richard, Duke of York. He held his title in right of his wife, Alice Montacute, 5th Countess of Salisbury. During York's Protectorate, Salisbury was appointed as Lord Chancellor. He was swiftly displaced from office when York's Protectorate ended with Henry VI's return to such level of mental capacity as he had exhibited before his illness. Salisbury was present at the first Battle of St Albans, where they captured Henry VI. Not yet thinking of claiming the Crown, York, supported by Salisbury and the others, renewed their allegiance to Henry. Salisbury took part, arm-in-arm, with Somerset, in the Loveday procession supposed to indicate the restoration of amity between Henry and York. In September 1459 Salisbury took his troops to meet York at Ludlow. En route, Salisbury and his men achieved a victory at Blore Heath. At Ludlow however, they did not have sufficient men who were prepared to fight directly against the King. Salisbury together with Warwick and the young Edward, Earl of March escaped to Calais. He returned to England with the rest of the Yorkist Lords in 1460, and was killed at the Battle of Wakefield along with his brother-in-law York and his nephew Rutland.

**Neville, Richard, Earl of Warwick 22 November 1428 – 14 April 1471** Known to history as Warwick the Kingmaker, Warwick was a leading participant in the Wars of the Roses, first for York, and when he discovered that he was unable to rule his cousin, Edward IV, as the defender of Lancaster. Warwick was the son of Richard Neville, Earl of Salisbury. He married Anne Beauchamp, 16th Countess of Warwick, and, as was the custom, held her lands and title. Warwick, like his father, Salisbury, was an early supporter of York. It was Warwick's men who began hostilities at the first Battle of St Albans and overpowered royalist forces. Following the battle in an effort to show their loyalty to Henry VI, York, Salisbury and Warwick all accompanied him to a ceremony at St Paul's at which

Warwick bore the King's sword. During York's second Protectorate, Warwick was appointed as Captain of Calais, a post which he retained even after York was dismissed. At the Loveday procession Warwick made a show of reconciliation with the Duke of Exeter, husband of his cousin, Anne of York. With his control of Calais, Warwick became a key player. He rendezvoused with York at Ludlow but, when it became apparent that the Yorkists could not fight the royal army he escaped, together with his cousin, Edward, Earl of March, to Calais. The following year, he led an invasion force which overwhelmed the Lancastrians at the Battle of Northampton, where Henry VI was captured. This was followed by the Lancastrian victory at the second Battle of St Albans. Warwick, escaping, took the remnants of his army to meet Edward of York, who now had himself proclaimed King. For the first few years of Edward's reign Warwick was, or considered himself to be, the second most important man in the kingdom.

Eventually, he quarrelled with Edward when it became apparent that Edward was his own man. In particular Warwick was humiliated when his negotiations with France for a marriage between Edward and a French princess came to nothing because Edward had secretly married Elizabeth Woodville. Warwick bore a grudge and four years later in 1469, attempted to take control of government by holding Edward captive. This scheme did not work out and Warwick decided on a last-ditch attempt to maintain power by reconciling himself with his old enemy, Margaret of Anjou, and reinstating Henry VI as King. Edward IV escaped to exile in Burgundy for about a year but then returned and annihilated Warwick's army at the Battle of Barnet. Warwick was killed.

**Neville, Sir Thomas, d. 30 December 1460** The marriage of Sir Thomas Neville, son of Richard, Earl of Salisbury to Maud Stanhope, gave rise to a battle between the Nevilles and the Percys, fuelling further rounds of baronial dispute that underlay the Wars of the Roses. Neville was killed alongside his father at the battle of Wakefield.

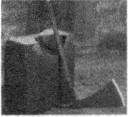 **Neville, Thomas, Bastard of Fauconberg, 1429 – 20 to September 1471** The illegitimate son of William, Lord Fauconberg, Neville adhered to his cousin Warwick, and even after the Lancastrian defeat at Tewkesbury he attempted to hold London for the Lancastrians. He was defeated but escaped. Following his later capture, he was executed.

**Neville, William, Baron Fauconberg, circa 1405 – 9 January 1463** The son of Ralph Neville 1st Earl of Westmorland by second wife Joan Beaufort, he married Joan, 6th Baroness Fauconberg. He was with the Lancastrian army at the first Battle of St Albans but moved increasingly into the Yorkist camp. He was one of the Yorkist commanders at the Battles of Northampton, second St Albans, and Towton. Edward IV ennobled him as 1st Earl of Kent.

**Norris, Thomas, Captain of Beaumaris** In 1450 Norris received orders from Henry VI that York and his men would be delayed on their return from Ireland.

# O

**Ogle, Sir Robert, 1406 – 1469** A leader of a Yorkist contingent at the first Battle of St Albans.

**Oldhall, Sir William, c.1390 – 1460** A veteran of the French wars, Oldhall became Chamberlain to the Duke of York in around 1440. He became Speaker of the House of Commons in 1450. As a proxy in Somerset and York's private war, Oldhall was accused by Walter de Burgh of having taken part in a riot resulting in the looting of Somerset's house. Oldhall fled into sanctuary at St Martin's le Grand, but was dragged out by a party of nobles, including Salisbury and the Earl of Wiltshire. Such a breach of sanctuary could not be tolerated and Oldhall was returned to the church, where he remained trapped for some three years.

## Paston to Swynford

# P

**Paston, Clement** A member of the Paston family of Norfolk, his letters give information about the state of London in the winter 1460 – 61.

**Paston, John** A member of the Paston family of Norfolk, he was advised by his brother Clement, studying in London, to be prepared for battle at any moment as the political situation deteriorated in 1460 – 61.

**Percy, Henry, 2ⁿᵈ Earl of Northumberland, three February 1393 – 22 May 1455** The feud between the Percy and the Neville families was one of the underlying causes of the Wars of the Roses. Northumberland, although married to Eleanor Neville and thus, brother-in-law to York, who was married to Eleanor's sister, Cecily, continued in the traditional Percy loyalty to Lancaster. He was killed at the first Battle of St Albans.

**Percy, Henry, 3ʳᵈ Earl of Northumberland, 25 July 1421 – 29 March 1461** Northumberland, whose father had been killed supporting Henry VI at the first Battle of St Albans, nursed a grudge against the Yorkists. He took part in the Loveday parade which was intended to reconcile those who had lost fathers and brothers at the battle to each other. Unfortunately, it did not. The 3ʳᵈ Earl was killed fighting for Lancaster at Towton.

**Percy, Henry 4ᵗʰ Earl of Northumberland, 1449 – 28 April 1489** 12 years old when his father was killed at Towton, fighting for Lancaster, Henry was eventually reconciled to Edward IV and re-established in the earldom of Northumberland. During Edward's reign he worked with Richard, Duke of Gloucester, to hold the North. Gloucester was perceived by many to be the heir of the Neville influence in the North which had always been inimical to the Percys.  Whether it was this or some other unknown factor, cannot be known but, after initially accepting Richard III as King, Northumberland brought his troops to Bosworth but declined to fight. After brief imprisonment at the beginning of Henry VII's reign, he was restored to all of his honours but was lynched in 1489 when attempting to collect taxes.

**Percy, Sir Ralph, d 1464** A son of Henry Percy 2nd Earl of Northumberland, Percy was a Lancastrian, superficially reconciled to Edward IV but determined on revenge for the death of his father and brother.  He died fighting for Lancaster at the Battle of Hedgeley Moor.

**Percy, Thomas, Lord Egremont, 29 November 1422 – 10 July 1460** Egremont led an ambush at the marriage of Sir Thomas Neville and Maud Stanhope as part of the ongoing feud between the Nevilles and Percys.  He fought for Lancaster at the Battle of Northampton and was amongst those Lords who were deliberately killed following the battle.

**Philip the Bold, Duke of Burgundy, 17 January 1342 – 27 April 1404** Uncle of the mentally incapacitated Charles VI of France, Burgundy fought a bloody war with his nephew, Louis of Orleans, for control of the King.  He allied with the English, and this fatally weakened France in the face of English aggression.

**Philip the Good, Duke of Burgundy, 31 July 1396 – 15 June 1467** In 1435 Philip, following two generations of civil strife, came to terms with Charles VII of France at the Treaty of Arras.  In return for the King finding and punishing the assassins of Philip's father, John the Fearless, Philip would abandon the Burgundian alliance with England. Philip had an astonishing three wives and 24 mistresses, producing some 21 children in all.

**Philip the Fair, Duke of Burgundy, 22 July 1478 – 25 September 1506** Philip was the son of Mary, Duchess of Burgundy and the Emperor Maximilian. He inherited the duchy on his mother's death when he was only four years old. At the age of 18 he was married to Joanna, daughter of Ferdinand of Aragon and Isabella of Castile. In 1501 Henry VII travelled to Calais where he met Duke Philip and agreed a treaty. In 1506 the rulers met again when Philip and Joanna were travelling to claim her inheritance, the throne of Castile, and were shipwrecked in England. They remained as honoured guests until Maximilian was persuaded to hand over Edmund de la Pole to Henry VII. Philip did not long enjoy his wife's crown, dying suddenly at the age of 28.

**Philip III, King of France, 30 April 1245 – 5 October 1285** Son of Louis IX and Margaret of Provence, Philip's daughter by his second marriage, Margaret of France, was the second wife of Edward I, and ancestress of both Anne Boleyn and Catherine Howard. By his first marriage Philip III was grand-father of Isabella of France, through whom Edward III claimed the French throne.

**Philip IV, King of France, 1268 – 29 November 1314** Father through his wife Joanna, Queen of Navarre, of Isabella of France, Queen of England, through whom the English Kings claimed the Crown of France.

**Philip V, King of France, 1291 – 3 January 1322** He supported his sister, Isabella of France, and his nephew, Prince Edward, with men and troops to overthrow Isabella's husband, Edward II of England.

**Plantagenet, Arthur, Viscount Lisle d. 1542** Lisle was an illegitimate son of Edward IV and thus half-uncle to Henry VIII. In 1501, he joined the household of his half-sister, Queen Elizabeth of York, and then transferred to that of Henry VII. He received many offices under Henry VIII, including Vice-Admiral of the Fleet, and, in 1533 was appointed Governor of Calais. The massive correspondence that remains from Lisle and his household give many of the details of Henry's court in the 1530s. In 1540, it was alleged that a plot was afoot to surrender Calais to the French. Lisle was arrested and imprisoned. After two years, as no evidence had been found against him, it was decided to release him, but, unfortunately, on hearing the good news he died of a heart attack.

**Plantagenet, Lady Margaret, Countess of Salisbury 14 April 1473 – 27 May 1541** Margaret was the niece of Edward IV and thus first cousin to Elizabeth of York. A marriage was arranged for her to Sir Richard Pole, a Tudor supporter and half-nephew of Margaret Beaufort, and she remained within Court circles during Henry VII's reign. Margaret became a close friend of Katherine of Aragon, and was godmother and Lady Governess to Henry VIII and Katharine's daughter, Mary. Her title of Countess of Salisbury was heritable through the female line, and it was restored, together with some of the lands, in 1512. Margaret remained at the centre of Court life until the annulment suit began, although she had a rather chequered relationship with Henry. Margaret sided with her friend, Katharine, as far possible, but did not openly disobey Henry and wrote firmly to her rebellious son, Reginald Pole, in Rome, chastising him for criticising the King. Nevertheless, Margaret and her other sons were suspected of treason during the Exeter Conspiracy. She was arrested in 1538 and sent to the Tower. Attainted of treason, and with her lands and titles again confiscated, she remained there, protesting ignorance of the cause of her imprisonment, until 1541 when she was executed in a botched beheading.

**Plumpton, Sir William, 1404 – 15 October 1480** A retainer of the Percys', Plumpton was summoned to join the Lancastrian army in March 1461. He fought and survived the Battle of Towton; his son was not so fortunate. Eventually reconciled to Edward of York, Plumpton regained his offices.

**Pole, Edmund de la, 3rd Duke of Suffolk, c. 1472 – 30 April 1514** Only 13 at the time of Bosworth, Edmund was a frequent visitor to the court of his cousin, Queen Elizabeth of York, and Henry VII.  He supported Henry throughout the Perkin Warbeck affair and against the Cornish rebels.  However financially embarrassed, and perhaps mindful that many people believed he was the rightful king, he left England without permission in 1499.  He was sent home and obliged to pay a large fine but he had now attracted the King's suspicions.  In November 1501 he and his brother Richard again left England without permission and travelled to the court of the Holy Roman Emperor, Maximilian.  Maximilian delighted at this new opportunity to keep other European rulers on their toes, paraded Suffolk about as King of England.  Unfortunately for Suffolk, in 1506, Maximilian's son, Philip the Fair of Burgundy and his wife Joanna of Castile, were shipwrecked in England.  It was soon apparent that Philip would continue to enjoy Henry's hospitality for as long as Suffolk enjoyed Maximilian's.  Suffolk was returned to England on the promise that his life would be spared.  Henry VII kept his word to the letter and merely imprisoned Suffolk in the Tower of London.  Henry VIII had no such fine feelings, and Suffolk was executed when Henry was preparing to go to war in France in 1513.

**Pole, Humphrey de la, 1474 – 1513** A younger son of John, 2nd Duke of Suffolk, fortunately for Humphrey he was in holy orders and therefore exempt from the suspicions of treason which fell on his brothers.

**Pole, John de la** Brother of William de la Pole, 1st Duke of Suffolk.

**Pole, John de la, 2nd Duke of Suffolk, 27 September 1442 – c. 1492** In his early youth John was married to Lady Margaret Beaufort, later Countess of Richmond, but the marriage was dissolved before it was completed.  When he was eight, his father was killed, and he was transferred to the wardship of Richard, Duke of York. He married York's daughter, Elizabeth, and became a warm adherent of his father-in-law. He was demoted to the rank of Earl in the Coventry Parliament following the Yorkist loss at Ludford Bridge. He fought for York at the second Battle of St Albans and was an important member of the Royal family once Edward IV became King, having his dukedom restored. He and Elizabeth had eleven children but no grandchildren. The eldest son John, Earl of Lincoln was probably named by Richard III as his heir after the death of Edward of Middleham, Prince of Wales. Following the Battle of Bosworth, Suffolk took no part in the Yorkist rebellion of 1487 in which his son was killed.

**Pole, John de la, Earl of Lincoln, c 1462 – 16 June 1487** Son of Elizabeth of York and John, 2nd Duke of Suffolk, Lincoln supported his uncle, Richard III, and was granted a place on the Council of the North. It is likely that Richard considered Lincoln as his heir. Although reconciled to Henry VII following the Battle of Bosworth, two years later Lincoln played a leading part in the Lambert Simnel affair, being present at the coronation of the boy. Lincoln was killed at the Battle of Stoke.

**Pole, Katherine de la, Abbess of Barking** Sister of William de la Pole, Duke of Suffolk. In 1437, Edmund and Jasper Tudor, the children of Queen Catherine de Valois by her second marriage, were entrusted to her care.

**Pole, Richard de la, 1480 – 24 February 1524** De la Pole secretly left England in 1501 together with his brother Edmund. He spent the rest of his life on the Continent, being passed around the courts of Europe amongst those rulers who wished to provoke the Kings of England. He was killed at the Battle of Pavia, fighting in the French army.

**Pole, William de la, 4th Earl and 1st Duke of Suffolk, c. 1396 – 1450** In 1428, Suffolk took over command of the English forces at Orleans, following the death of the Earl of Salisbury. He was utterly routed by the appearance of Joan of Arc. On his return to England he became a member of the King's Council and gradually rose in influence and importance. He was initially effective in government because he had a good relationship both with Cardinal Beaufort, and Humphrey, Duke of Gloucester. He negotiated the truce with France that resulted in the marriage of Henry VI to Margaret of Anjou. This truce was considered dishonourable by the War Party as it involved not just marriage to a girl with an insignificant dowry but also the ceding of the county of Maine. Over the following years Suffolk became increasingly unpopular with both Lords and Commons. In the Parliament of January 1450 he was impeached. Permitted to plead his case before the King, he pointed out his many years of service to the Crown. Henry VI found him guilty, not of the greater counts of treason that had been brought, but of lesser crimes, and sentenced him to five years of banishment. As Suffolk left England, his ship was captured by a craft called the *Nicholas of the Tower,* Suffolk was dragged on-board and executed with a rusty sword.

**Pole, William de la, 1478 – c. 1539** Son of John, 2nd Duke of Suffolk, William was imprisoned in the Tower when his brothers secretly left England in 1501. He remained there for the rest of his life.

**Pole, Sir Geoffrey c. 1502 – 1558** Pole was the younger son of Margaret Plantagenet, Countess of Salisbury and younger brother of Cardinal Reginald Pole. His evidence about correspondence between his mother and brother, Lord Montague, with Cardinal Pole was the foundation for the charges of treason laid against Montague, the Countess, and their cousin, Henry Courtenay, Marquess of Exeter. Sir Geoffrey pleaded guilty to charges of treason in 1538, and was pardoned in 1539.  After his mother's execution, he left England for Rome, returning at the accession of Mary I.

 **Pole, Henry, 1st Baron Montague, c. 1492 – 9 January 1536** The oldest son and heir of Lady Margaret Plantagenet, Countess of Salisbury, he was on good terms with his cousin Henry VIII until his father-in-law, Edward Stafford, 3rd Duke of Buckingham was executed for treason.  Montague spent a short period in the Tower of London but was then released and apparently restored to favour.  He supported Henry's annulment of his first marriage, but by the late 1530s the King was becoming increasingly suspicious of Montague and their mutual cousin, the Marquess of Exeter.  Montague was accused of treason and executed.

**Pole, Reginald, Cardinal, 1500 - 1558** Pole was the son of Margaret Plantagenet, Countess of Salisbury, and was Henry VIII's second cousin.  Pole's education was initially paid for by Henry, and he had a very promising career until the matter of the annulment of the King's marriage arose.  Pole was a staunch defender of the power of the Pope and of the Catholic Church, although his personal theology reflected the humanist trend of the early sixteenth century.  His support of the Pope and his nearness to the throne rendered Pole one of Henry's deadliest enemies, especially when he called upon European princes to depose the King.  In 1538 Pole's brother, mother and cousin were arrested and imprisoned on charges of treason and two of them later executed.  In 1556 Pole was ordained priest and became the last Catholic Archbishop of Canterbury, under Mary I.

 **Poynings, Sir Robert. c. 1419 – 17 February 1461** Poynings supported the rebellion of Jack Cade.  He died fighting for York at the second Battle of St Albans.

**Poynings, Sir Edward, 1459 – 22 October 1521**  Poynings, after initial involvement in Buckingham's rebellion in 1483, escaped to Brittany where he joined Henry Tudor.  Following the coronation of Henry VII he joined the King's Privy Council and became Lord Deputy of Ireland.  Part of his duties were to contain Irish support for Perkin Warbeck.

# Q

**Quelennec, Jean du, Admiral of Brittany**  In 1472 Jasper Tudor, Earl of Pembroke and his nephew Henry, were maintained in the Château of du Quelennec, on the orders of Duke Francis II of Brittany.

# R

**Radcliffe, John, 8th Baron FitzWalter, d. April 1471**  A Yorkist Lord killed in the skirmishes at Ferrybridge, before the Battle of Towton.

**Radcliffe, John, 9th Baron FitzWalter, 1452 – c. 24 November 1496**  During the reign of Henry VII he was involved in the Perkin Warbeck rebellion, and attainted.  He was not initially executed but when he attempted to escape from prison in Calais he was beheaded.

**Ratcliffe, Sir Richard d. 22 August 1485**  One of Richard III's closest associates, the second in the old rhyme *'the cat, the rat, and Lovell the dog, rule all England under a hog'*, he was killed at the Battle of Bosworth.

**René I, Duke of Anjou, Bar, Lorraine, King of Naples, Jerusalem and Sicily. January 1409 – 1480**  Despite his many grand titles, René was perpetually broke and unlucky in war.   His daughter, Margaret, became the wife of Henry VI of England.

**Richard, 3rd Duke of York, 21 September 1411 – 30 December 1460**   Richard embodied two claims to the throne of England, one through his mother's descent from Lionel, Duke of Clarence, second son of Edward III, and the other through his paternal descent from Edmund, Duke of York, of Edward III. Following the execution of his father for rebellion against Henry IV, York had been granted as a ward to Ralph Neville, first Earl of Westmorland. He married Westmorland's daughter, Cecily, in 1429 and they had a large family. York, like all of the other men of his generation, fought in France. He was appointed as Lord Lieutenant of Normandy and had some success there.   Unfortunately, however, he was locked in a bitter rivalry with the Duke of Somerset, another royal cousin. Somerset was favoured by Henry VI and Margaret of Anjou, and this led to York feeling that he was not being given the position in government that his seniority merited.   On York's return from France, he was appointed in 1447 as Lord Lieutenant of Ireland for a period of 10 years which, more or less, amounted to banishment.   Having left England only in 1449, York returned without permission in 1450 to a country rapidly descending into chaos. Henry VI refused his request to become his most senior minister, merely inviting him to join the King's Council.

When the King fell into a catatonic stupor, York was given the position of Lord Protector, much to the disgruntlement of Somerset.   During this period he seems to have made attempts to govern fairly and without excessive preference of his own supporters, although he did have Somerset confined to the Tower.   When Henry VI regained his senses, York was dismissed and much of his work undone.   Matters went from bad to worse and eventually York took up arms against the King at the first Battle of St Albans. Following the battle, York was eager to prove that he had no dishonourable intentions and reaffirmed his loyalty to the King. Unfortunately matters did not improve and following the Battle of Northampton in 1460, Richard claimed the throne himself. The other Lords would not agree, however it was decided that whilst Henry would remain King the rest of his life, Richard would be his successor, disinheriting Henry's young son, Edward of Lancaster. This was never going to be acceptable to Queen Margaret and many other Lancastrian supporters. Open war broke out and Richard and his second son, Edmund, Earl of Rutland, were killed at the Battle of Wakefield on 30 December 1460. Jones' portrait of the Duke of York is of a man with good intentions but blinded by his own self-importance.

**Richard II, King of England, 6 January 1367 – c. 14 February 1400** The son of Edward, the Black Prince, Richard inherited the throne from his grandfather, Edward III, in 1377 when he was just 10. He showed great personal courage at the age of 14 when he faced down the Peasants Revolt but he became increasingly tyrannical as his reign progressed. He was deposed (and probably murdered, although he may have committed suicide) by his cousin, Henry of Bolingbroke, who reigned as Henry IV. Richard had married twice but had no children, and had named as his heir, Edmund, Earl of March, the grandson of Edward III's second son, Lionel, Duke of Clarence. March transmitted his claim to his own great-nephew, Richard, Duke of York.

**Richard III, King of England, October 1452 – 22 August 1485** Richard was the youngest son of Richard, Duke of York, and Cecily Neville. He spent much of his childhood in the care of his cousin, Richard Neville, Earl of Warwick. Given the title of Duke of Gloucester, he was a loyal lieutenant to his brother, Edward IV, but quarrelled with his other brother, George, Duke of Clarence, over the inheritance of their wives, who were sisters. Richard played a leading part in the Battles of Barnet and of Tewkesbury. He acted as the King's lieutenant in the North during Edward IV's reign, in an uneasy relationship with Henry Percy, Duke of Northumberland. On Edward's death, Richard, warned by Lord Hastings that the new King Edward V's maternal relatives, the Woodvilles, intended to dominate a new government, headed swiftly towards London. He met the young Edward V at Stony Stratford, and arrested the boy's uncle, Anthony Woodville, Earl Rivers, and his half-brother, Sir Richard Grey. Richard, having sworn fealty to Edward, proceeded to London. It was agreed that Richard would take the position of Lord Protector. The King's Coronation was postponed for some weeks but never took place. Richard announced that the marriage of Edward IV and Elizabeth Woodville had been invalid and that therefore Edward V and his siblings were illegitimate. He was crowned as Richard III on 22 June 1483. Almost immediately rebellions broke out, the most significant being that led by his erstwhile supporter Henry Stafford, 2nd Duke of Buckingham. This was quashed. Richard invested his son, Edward of Middleham, as Prince of Wales, but was heartbroken when the boy, his only legitimate child, died on 4 April 1484. He was aware that many supporters of his late brother were leaving England to join the Lancastrian claimant, Henry Tudor, in Brittany. In the summer of 1485 Richard, anticipating an invasion, summoned his troops to Leicester. On 22 August, Richard was defeated and killed at the Battle of Bosworth. *If you want to know what Jones thinks happened to Edward V and his brother, you will have to read his book!*

**Richard of Shrewsbury, Duke of York, 17 August 1483 – probably summer 1485** Richard was the second son of Edward IV and Elizabeth Woodville. When it became apparent that his 12-year-old brother, Edward V, would be dominated by his uncle, Richard, Duke of Gloucester, Queen Elizabeth took Richard and his sisters into sanctuary in Westminster Abbey. She was persuaded to release the boy, who joined his brother in the Tower of London and was never seen again.

**Rieux, Jean de, Marshal of Brittany** De Rieux had custody of Henry Tudor in Brittany at the Tour d'Elven.

**Robesart, Louis de** One of the guardians of Henry VI during his early childhood.

**Robin of Redesdale** A mysterious figure who led a series of uprisings in the North of England in the spring of 1469. It seems likely that even if the first Robin of Redesdale were genuine, later rioting under his name was stirred up by the Earl of Warwick and his associates as a way to suggest that they had legitimate grievances against Edward IV's government.

 **Roos, de, Thomas, 9th Baron de Roos** One of the leaders of the Lancastrians at the Battle of Wakefield, he went into exile with Henry VI and Margaret of Anjou following the Battle of Towton. He returned to fight for Lancaster at both Hedgeley Moor and the Battle of Hexham on 15 May 1464. He was captured and executed.

**Rotherham, Thomas, Archbishop of York, 24 August 1423 – 29 May 1500** Rotherham was appointed as Lord Chancellor under Edward IV, amongst other positions. On Edward IV's death he handed the great seal over to Elizabeth Woodville, although it was later recovered from her. Rotherham was arrested at the same time as Lord Hastings was executed, and imprisoned in the Tower for some weeks. During the reign of Henry VII he lived largely in retirement.

# S

**Savage, Sir John**   A retainer of Sir William Stanley, declared by Richard III to be a traitor shortly before the Battle of Bosworth. Savage fought for Henry Tudor at the battle, to the left of the Earl of Oxford.

**Scales, Thomas, 7<sup>th</sup> Baron Scales, 1397 – 25 July 1460**   Scales fought in France under John of Lancaster, Duke of Bedford. Together with Matthew Gough he attempted to defend London against Jack Cade's rebels.

**Schwartz, Martin, d. 16 June 1487**   Leader of a mercenary force hired by the Yorkists to support the pretender Lambert Simnel. He was killed at the Battle of Stoke.

**Scrope, Margaret**   The granddaughter of Henry Scrope, 4th Baron Scrope of Bolton, she was the wife of Edmund de la Pole, 3<sup>rd</sup> Duke of Suffolk.

**Shaa, Dr Ralph. d. 1484**   On 22 June 1483 Doctor Shaa preached at St Paul's Cross. He announced that the marriage between Edward IV and Elizabeth Woodville had been invalid as, he alleged, the King had previously been betrothed to Lady Eleanor Butler (née Talbot).

**Simonds, William**   The tutor of Lambert Simnel.

**Simnel, Lambert, circa 1477 – after 1525**   Lambert Simnel, whose real name is uncertain, first burst onto the historical scene in 1487 when as a boy of about 10, he was crowned as King Edward VI in Christchurch, Dublin.   It was alleged that he was Edward, Earl of Warwick, son of George, Duke of Clarence. As the real Earl of Warwick was firmly locked up in the Tower of London, this was clearly impossible.   Nevertheless unreconciled Yorkists, led by John de la Pole, Earl of Lincoln, Francis, Lord Lovell and Margaret of York, Dowager Duchess of Burgundy, staged the impersonation.   It is unclear what was intended to happen to Simnel, had Henry VII's forces been defeated.   It is difficult to imagine that the

Yorkist Lords intended he should actually be King. The Yorkists raised an army and invaded England in the North West. They marched to Stoke in Staffordshire and were roundly defeated under an army led by Henry VII in person. Simnel himself was treated kindly. After a brief sojourn in the Tower, he was given a job in the royal kitchens and eventually promoted to falconer.

**Simnel, Thomas**  An Oxfordshire carpenter, possibly the father of Lambert Simnel.

**Shakespeare, William c 26 April 1564 – 23 April 1616** Shakespeare's cycle of plays about the Wars of the Roses have influenced our interpretation ever since. The title of Jones work, *'The Hollow Crown'* is derived from Act III Sc. ii of *'The Life and Death of Richard II'*, first performed in 1595.

**Shore, Elizabeth (Jane) c 1445 – 1527** Elizabeth was the daughter of one London merchant and the wife of another. She became the mistress of Edward IV in around 1476 and was still his lover at the time of his death. Edward seems to have been genuinely attached to her. She was also the mistress of Edward's friend, William, Lord Hastings and the King's stepson, Thomas, Marquess of Dorset. Elizabeth was forced to do public penance by Richard III, but then married his Solicitor General, Thomas Lynom.

**Somerset, John**  Henry VI's doctor during his childhood.

**Stacey, Master John, d. 19 May 1477** A Fellow of Merton College, Oxford, Stacey was accused, together with Thomas Blake and Thomas Burdet, of predicting the King's death using sorcery. He was hanged on 19 May 1477. George, Duke of Clarence, proclaimed the men's innocence in front of the Privy Council.

**Stafford, Sir Henry, c. 1425 – October 1471** Second son of Humphrey Stafford, 1st Duke of Buckingham, Stafford was married to the widowed Lady Margaret Beaufort, Countess of Richmond in 1458. He fought for Lancaster at Towton, but was subsequently reconciled to Edward IV. In 1471, Stafford was forced to choose between his old Lancastrian loyalty and Edward IV. He chose Edward IV and fought at the Battle of Barnet for York. He was severely wounded and died in October of that year.

**Stafford, Henry, 2nd Duke of Buckingham, 4 September 1454 – 2 November 1483** Grandson of the 1st Duke of Buckingham, when his father was killed for Lancaster at the Battle of Towton, Buckingham was recognised as Duke and given in wardship to loyal Yorkists, including eventually, Queen Elizabeth Woodville. He was married to her sister Katharine, which he apparently perceived to be an insult to his Royal blood. On the death of Edward IV, he supported Richard III, for which he received recognition in the form of the restoration of the de Bohun estates of his ancestor, Eleanor de Bohun, Duchess of Gloucester. Not long after Richard's coronation however, Buckingham began to plot rebellion. It is unclear whether he was aiming to replace Richard with Henry Tudor or, more likely, with himself. His efforts were a failure, and, betrayed by one of his own men, he was captured by Richard III and executed.

**Stafford, Humphrey, 1st Duke of Buckingham, 15 August 1402 – 10 July 1460** Buckingham was the grandson of Edward III's youngest son, Thomas, Duke of Gloucester. In around 1424, he married Anne Neville, daughter of the 1st Earl of Westmorland and Joan Beaufort. He was created Duke of Buckingham in 1444 with precedence over all non-royal dukes. In 1450 he, along with others, was sent to quash Jack Cade's rebellion in Kent, but before they arrived, the rebels had marched on London. Buckingham remained loyal to Henry VI. He negotiated for the royalist party at the first Battle of St Albans but to no avail. He commanded Lancastrian forces at the Battle of Nottingham. Not actually killed in the battle, he was executed by the victorious Yorkists immediately thereafter.

**Stafford, Humphrey, 1st Earl of Devon c. 1439 – 17 August 1469** Stafford was a distant relative of the Dukes of Buckingham. He fought for York at the Battles of Mortimer's Cross and Towton. A supporter of Edward IV, he was granted the title of Earl of Devon, to replace the Courtenay earls, who were Lancastrian. Whilst supporting Edward IV against Warwick's rebellion in 1469, he was murdered by a mob.

**Stafford, Sir Humphrey d. 1450** Sir Humphrey was killed attempting to put down Jack Cade's rebellion in 1450.

**Stafford, Sir William d. 1450** Sir William was killed with his kinsman, Sir Humphrey, near Tonbridge in Kent, attempting to put down Jack Cade's rebellion

**Stanhope, Maud, d. after 1463** Maud's second marriage in 1453 to Sir Thomas Neville, son of Richard, Earl of Salisbury, was the occasion of a private battle between the Percys and the Nevilles.

**Stanley, Thomas, Lord Stanley, Earl of Derby, c. 1435 – 29 July 1504** Thomas Stanley achieved the amazing feat of never fighting at any of the battles of the Wars of the Roses. At the encounter at Blore Heath, he held his army back, which probably contributed to the Yorkist victory. He brought men in support of Warwick at the beginning of the Lancastrian resurgence in 1469 but they were not deployed, as Edward IV did not give battle. In 1472, he married the wealthy widow Lady Margaret Beaufort, Countess of Richmond. Stanley became a faithful supporter of Edward IV, being appointed Lord Steward. He supported his wife in her efforts to have her son, Henry Tudor, brought home from exile and reconciled to Edward IV. Before this could happen Edward died and Stanley was faced with the question of whether to support Richard III. Initially, he did so. His wife however, did not. When Lady Margaret was attainted for her part in the rebellion of the Duke of Buckingham, her lands were granted to her husband, who was supposed to keep her under house arrest.

When Henry Tudor landed in Wales in August 1485 it is unclear whether Stanley had committed to supporting him or not. Stanley's eldest son, George, Lord Strange, was being held hostage by Richard III. Stanley brought a large army towards Bosworth and had at least one secret meeting with his stepson before the battle. Nevertheless once hostilities commenced he did nothing. Following the battle it is alleged he crowned his stepson on the field. Henry granted his stepfather the title of Earl of Derby.

 **Stanley, Sir William, c. 1435 – 10 February 1495** Like his older brother, Thomas, Lord Stanley, Sir William avoided all of the battles of the Wars of the Roses until the Battle of Bosworth. He was present with his brother on the outskirts of the encounter at Blore Heath, and sent some men to relieve the Yorkist Earl of Salisbury, but did not commit himself further. Richard III suspected his loyalty and declared him a traitor prior to the Battle of Bosworth. At the battle William watched from the sidelines as events unfolded, and only after Richard III had made his last headlong advance towards Henry Tudor, did Stanley bring in his troops in support of his brother's stepson. Stanley was rewarded with the post of Lord Chamberlain, but became suspected of involvement in the Perkin Warbeck plot. He was tried and executed on 16 February 1495.

**Stillington, Robert Bishop of Bath and Wells, 1420 – 1491** It has been alleged that it was Bishop Stillington who told Richard III about a pre-contract of marriage between Lady Eleanor Butler (née Talbot) and Edward IV, impugning the legality of Edward's marriage to Elizabeth

Woodville. Stillington became involved in the Lambert Simnel rebellion, and died in prison.

**Stanley, George, Lord Strange, 1460 – 1503** In 1482, Stanley was married to Joan, 9th Baroness Strange, a niece of Elizabeth Woodville, and granted a number of offices by Edward IV. At the time of the Battle of Bosworth he was held hostage by Richard III, for the good behaviour of his father, Thomas, Lord Stanley. Infuriated that the Stanleys had not joined him, Richard gave orders for Strange to be executed. The orders were not carried out. He became a Privy Councillor to Henry VII.

**Sutton, John, Baron Dudley 25 December 1400 – 30 September 1487** Lord Dudley was a standard-bearer at the funeral of Henry V. He was accused by the rebels of Jack Cade of treachery, along with other leading councillors of the King. He was taken prisoner together with the King at the first Battle of St Albans. Obviously unlucky, he was taken prisoner a second time by the Yorkists at the Battle of Blore Heath. By the time of Towton, however he had changed his allegiance, and fought for York.

**Swynford, Katherine, Duchess of Lancaster, 25 November 1349 – 10 May 1403** Katherine Swynford (née de Roet) was for many years the mistress of John of Gaunt, Duke of Lancaster, by whom she had four children, who were legitimised by Act of Parliament, following their parents' marriage. Their half-brother, Henry IV, added a clause barring them from succession to the Crown, however the validity of this is disputed. On the death of Lancaster's second Duchess, Constanza of Castile, he married Katherine. Through her son, John Beaufort, 1st Earl of Somerset, she is the ancestor of Henry VII and all of the Kings of Scotland from James II onward. Through her daughter Joan Beaufort, Countess of Westmorland, Katherine is the ancestor of Edward IV and Richard III.

## Talbot to Young

### T

**Talbot, John, first Earl of Shrewsbury, circa 1384 – 17 July 1453** Known as *'Old Talbot'*, Shrewsbury was one of the most experienced English commanders in France. In his early career he had fought with Henry IV against Owain Glyndwr's insurgency, and later held the post of Lord Lieutenant of Ireland. It was at Shrewsbury's orders that a detailed family tree showing Henry VI's valid claim to the throne of France was created. He achieved many notable victories against the French during his career but was killed at the Battle of Castillon, which destroyed England's centuries' long hold of Aquitaine. He was the father of Lady Eleanor Butler, alleged to have been secretly pre-contracted to marry Edward IV.

**Tempest, John** Tempest attempted, but failed, to capture Henry VI in July 1465, when the deposed king was in hiding in the North of England.

**Tempest, Sir Richard of Waddington Hall** He hid the fugitive Henry VI in July 1465.

**Thomas of Lancaster, Duke of Clarence, before 25 November 1387 – 22 March 1421** The second son of Henry IV, he accompanied his brother, Henry V, throughout the King's campaigns in France. He was present at the Treaty of Troyes, and then remained in command in France whilst Henry V returned to England with his new bride, Catherine de Valois. In March 1421 he was killed in the Battle of Bauge, a serious defeat for the English army.

**Thomas of Woodstock, Duke of Gloucester, 7 January 1355 – 9 September 1397** The youngest son of Edward III, he was on very bad terms with his nephew, Richard II, being one of the Lords Appellant who sought to control Richard in 1388. Richard bided his time but when Gloucester was murdered at Calais in 1397, there was little doubt that it was at Richard's orders. Gloucester was the grandfather of Humphrey Stafford, 1st Duke of Buckingham.

**Thomas, David**  Like most of his family, David was a Lancastrian supporter. When his brother, Morgan Thomas, besieged Jasper, Earl of Pembroke and Henry Tudor in Pembroke Castle in 1471, David created a diversion enabling the Tudors to escape.

**Thomas, Morgan**  Although the Thomas family had been Lancastrian, Morgan Thomas changed sides when his father-in-law, Sir Roger Vaughan, was killed by Jasper Tudor, Earl of Pembroke. Thomas besieged Jasper and his , Henry Tudor, at Pembroke Castle in 1471.

**Thomas, Sir Rhys ap, 1449 – 1525**  Thomas was from a Lancastrian family that was forced into exile for a period early in the reign of Edward IV. Returning in 1467, Thomas and his family were apparently reconciled to York. He was given high office under Richard III, and declined to take part in Buckingham's rebellion. He was requested to send his son as a hostage to Richard III, but did not do so. When Henry Tudor invaded it was not clear whether Thomas would block his way or support him. In the event he chose to support Henry, and was at the Battle of Bosworth. He became one of Henry VII's Privy Councillors.

**Tiptoft, John, 1st Baron Tiptoft d. 27 January 1443**  A trusted servant and councillor of Henry V, he was one of the men responsible for the physical safety of the young Henry VI.

**Torrigiano, Pietro, 24 November 1472 – August 1528**  The master bronze sculptor who cast the effigies of Lady Margaret Beaufort, Countess of Richmond, Henry VII and Elizabeth of York over their tombs in Westminster Abbey.

**Trueblood, John, d. 1468** Trueblood was one of the defenders of Harlech Castle, which was besieged by the Yorkists between 1461 and 1468. When the Castle fell, Trueblood was taken to London with other members of the garrison and executed.

**Tuchet, James, 5th Baron Audley c. 1398 – 23 September 1459** A veteran of the French wars, he was a supporter of the Lancastrians, and in September 1459 received orders to prevent the Yorkist Earl of Salisbury rendezvousing with York and Warwick at Ludlow. He met with the Yorkists at the Battle of Blore Heath, but his forces were vanquished and Audley was killed.

**Tuchet, John, 6th Baron Audley, 1423 – 26 September 1490** Taken prisoner by the Yorkist Earl of Warwick, he was persuaded to transfer his allegiance from Lancaster to York. He fought for Edward IV at the battles of Northampton, Mortimer's Cross, Barnet and Tewkesbury and received a number of high offices in Edward's government.

**Tudor, Edmund, 1st Earl of Richmond, 11 June 1430 – 3 November 1456** Edmund was the first son born to Catherine de Valois, Dowager Queen of England, following her second marriage to Owen Tudor. After his mother's death, he and his siblings were put into the care of Katherine de la Pole, Abbess of Barking, and brought up at the expense of their half-brother, Henry VI. When Edmund was about 22, he was granted the earldom of Richmond and the hand of the wealthy child heiress Lady Margaret Beaufort. Initially on good terms with the Duke of York, he became embroiled in a turf war in South Wales with Sir William Herbert and Sir Walter Devereux, retainers of York's. As part of this feud, Edmund was imprisoned in Carmarthen Castle and died shortly after release, possibly of plague. He left a pregnant 13-year-old wife.

**Tudor, Jasper, Earl of Pembroke and Duke of Bedford, 1431 – 26 December 1495** The second son of Owen Tudor and Dowager Queen Catherine de Valois, he was granted the earldom of Pembroke by his half-brother, Henry VI. He fought energetically for Henry and was also a stalwart supporter of his widowed sister-in-law, Lady Margaret Beaufort, Countess of Richmond and his nephew, Henry Tudor. He lost the Battle of Mortimer's Cross, but escaped and joined the other Lancastrian exiles in Scotland. His earldom was granted to Sir William Herbert along with the wardship of Jasper's nephew, Henry Tudor. In 1468 he led a brief invasion but was forced to retreat. In 1469, when Warwick was attempting to put Henry VI back on the throne, Jasper was part of the invading army.

The following year, when Edward IV returned from exile, Jasper raised an army in Wales and was attempting to join up with the other Lancastrians, under Queen Margaret and Prince Edward of Lancaster, when the latter force was annihilated at Tewkesbury. Jasper and his nephew escaped across the channel to Brittany where they remained for nearly 14 years, before a brief spell in France, where the son of Jasper's cousin was now king. Jasper accompanied his nephew to Bosworth and was handsomely rewarded for his many years of loyalty. He was created Duke of Bedford and married to Catherine Woodville, sister of Queen Elizabeth Woodville and widow of Henry Stafford, 2$^{nd}$ Duke of Buckingham. Jasper had no children.

**Tudor, Katherine, c. 1437** A daughter of Catherine de Valois and Owen Tudor, who died in infancy.

**Tudor, Katherine, 2 February 1503 – 11 February 1503** The last child of Henry VII and Elizabeth of York, she died, along with her mother, a few days after her birth.

**Tudor, Owen, circa 1400 – 4 February 1461** Owen Tudor probably fought in France in the armies of Henry V, and became a member of the household of Henry's widow, Catherine de Valois. The couple married secretly despite a Parliamentary act forbidding anyone to marry the widowed Queen without specific consent from her adult son. On Catherine's death he attempted to return home to Wales but was detained and forced to return to London. After initially being released, he was again arrested and sent to prison in Newgate. He escaped Newgate but was again arrested and returned to custody in Windsor Castle eventually in 1439 he was released. He fought for his stepson Henry VI at the Battle of Mortimer's Cross. The victorious Yorkists captured him and he was executed in the marketplace at Hereford.

 **Twynho. Ankarette, d. 15 April 1479** Ankarette was a waiting woman to Isabel Neville, Duchess of Clarence. Two years after the Duchess' death, a band of retainers of her widower, George, Duke of Clarence, broke into Ankarette's home, in Somerset and took her by force to Warwick where she was tried and condemned for the murder of her mistress, two years previously. She was hanged immediately. There was no truth in the charge.

 **Tyrrell, Sir James c 1455 – 6 May 1502** Tyrrell was a retainer of Richard III, but absent from England at the time of Bosworth. In 1501 he was arrested for complicity in an alleged conspiracy surrounding Edmund de la Pole, 3rd Earl of Suffolk. He was executed and it was later claimed that, whilst in prison, he had confessed to the murder of Edward V and Richard of Shrewsbury Duke of York.

# V

 **Vaughan, Sir Roger, d. 1471** The Vaughans were supporters of Richard, Duke of York. Sir Roger fought at the Battle of Mortimer's Cross following which he was responsible for the execution of Owen Tudor. After Tewkesbury, Vaughan was sent to try to capture Jasper Tudor, Earl of Pembroke and

his nephew Henry Tudor. He was ambushed by Pembroke and executed in revenge for the death of Pembroke's father.

**Vaughan, Sir Thomas, d. June 1483** Chamberlain to Edward V, as Prince of Wales, he was accompanying the new King to London when the party was intercepted by Richard, Duke of Gloucester. Vaughan was arrested by Gloucester's men and was executed in June 1483.

**Vaux, Lady Katherine, née Peniston, d. after 1509** Lady-in-waiting to Queen Margaret of Anjou, Lady Vaux accompanied her through all her tribulations and was exiled with her in France. Following Margaret's death she returned to England and was granted pensions by both Edward IV and Richard III. On Henry VII's accession, Lady Vaux returned to court and played a full part in court ceremonial.

**Vergil, Polydore, c. 1470 – 18 April 1555** Vergil, a native of Urbino, was patronised by Henry VII, for whom he began his *Anglica Historia,* a major source for the history of the Wars of the Roses.

**Vere, Aubrey de, 20 February 1462** Son of the 12th Earl of Oxford, de Vere was accused of plotting against the life of Edward IV and executed.

**Vere, John de, 12th Earl of Oxford, 20 February 1462** Oxford took no part in the Wars of the Roses but in early 1462 he was accused of plotting against Edward IV and was executed.

**Vere, John de, 13th Earl of Oxford, 8 September 1442 – 10 March 1513** Although his father and brother had been executed for an alleged plot against Edward IV, Oxford was permitted to take up his inheritance and played a part in the Yorkist court. In 1469 he joined his brother-in-law, Richard Neville, Earl of Warwick, in rebellion against Edward IV and joined the Lancastrians in France. On the return of Henry VI, Oxford took part in the King's procession to St Paul's. He commanded one of the Lancastrian wings at Barnet but the similarity of his badge with that of Edward of York's sun-in-splendour led to confusion in the ranks of the Lancastrians leading them to turn on each other.   Oxford escaped and continued to attack Yorkist positions. Eventually captured was imprisoned in the fortress of Hammes near Calais from which he eventually escaped to join Henry Tudor in Brittany. Oxford was one of the leading commanders of Henry Tudor's forces at the Battle of Bosworth.  He remained one of Henry VII's most valued and trusted generals and councillors.

# W

**Warbeck, Perkin, c. 1474 – 23 November 1499**  Very little can be said with certainty as to the background of Pierrechon de Werebecq, but in 1491, he appeared in Cork, Ireland as the apprentice of a silk merchant.   Yorkist sympathisers claimed to recognise him as Richard of Shrewsbury, Duke of York, younger son of Edward IV.  The claim gained considerable support both at home and abroad.  Charles VIII of France, James IV of Scotland and Margaret, Dowager Duchess of Burgundy, who claimed to recognise Warbeck as her nephew.  All supported him financially.  After five years and a couple of failed invasions, Warbeck was captured by Henry VII's men.   He told the King that he was, in fact, the son of a Flemish merchant.  Henry VII, rather than executing him, kept him at the Royal Court and his wife, Lady Katherine Gordon, was amongst the Queen's ladies.   Perhaps tired of this silken imprisonment, Warbeck tried to escape and was sent to the Tower of London.  In 1499 he was tried for attempting to escape and hanged.

**Welles, Richard, 7th Baron Wells, d. 12 March 1470** Lord Welles and his son Sir Robert, were entangled in a local feud with Sir Thomas Burgh of Gainsborough, one of

Edward IV's bodyguard. On being told to desist, they ignored the King's orders, so the King marched against them. The rebels were routed at the Battle of Losecote Field. Lord Welles was killed.

**Welles, Sir Robert, 8th Baron Willoughby d'Eresby, d. 12 March 1470** The Willoughbys and the Burghs vied for pre-eminence in the county of Lincolnshire. This erupted into private warfare with Sir Thomas Burgh of Gainsborough, resulting in Edward IV bringing an army to quell the disturbances. Welles was killed at the Battle of Losecote Field.

**Wenlock, Sir John, first Baron Wenlock, c. 1400 – 1471** Wenlock fought for the Lancastrians at the first Battle of St Albans but then changed sides, and was with Salisbury's men at the Battle of Blore Heath, a Yorkist victory. He continued in his Yorkist loyalty through the battles of Mortimer's Cross, second battle of St Albans and Towton. Following Towton he was granted a barony. Wenlock was a close associate of the Earl of Warwick, and switched sides back to Lancaster with Warwick in 1469. He was one of the senior Lancastrian commanders at the Battle of Tewkesbury, and, like most of the others, was killed.

**Whethamstede, John, Abbot of St Albans** Following the second Battle of St Albans on 17 February 1461, the Abbot wrote of the shocking destruction wrought by the Lancastrian troops on the city.

**Wolsey, Thomas, Cardinal and Archbishop of York, c. 1470 – 29 November 1530** Wolsey was (probably) the son of an Ipswich grazier. Exceptionally intelligent, he graduated from Magdalen College, Oxford, aged just fifteen and was ordained priest in 1498. He entered the service of Henry VII in 1507 as Royal Chaplain, and secretary to Bishop Foxe, Lord Privy Seal. Wolsey was appointed Almoner to Henry VIII in 1509 and began a rapid climb to power. Wolsey was not just Henry VIII's Lord Chancellor, he had a warm personal relationship with the King, although he was never popular with Queen Katherine or the members of the nobility who considered him arrogant and proud. Wolsey lived in spectacular style, creating the masterpiece Hampton Court from a small manor house. He was an important figure in European politics, working with Henry to maintain a foreign policy that would enhance the prestige of England with the other European princes. Wolsey's failure to obtain an annulment of Henry's first marriage, and the personal animosity of Anne Boleyn, led to his catastrophic fall from power in 1529. Despite some dithering by Henry, he never regained influence, and in 1530 was accused of treason, dying en-route to London.

**Woodville, Anne, Lady Bourchier, circa 1438 – 30 July 1489** Sister of Queen Elizabeth Woodville.

**Woodville, Anthony, 2nd Earl Rivers, c. 1440 – 25 June 1483** Son of Sir Richard Woodville, and Jacquetta of Luxembourg, Duchess of Bedford, Woodville was a loyal Lancastrian, fighting at the Battle of Towton. After the Lancastrian defeat, following which his sister Elizabeth married the new King Edward IV, Woodville served his brother-in-law equally loyally. He was renowned both for his jousting skills and his piety. He lived the life of an ideal knight – fighting in tournaments, going on pilgrimage and promoting learning. He was a patron of the printer William Caxton. He was appointed as tutor to his nephew Edward, Prince of Wales and supervised the boy's education at Ludlow. When Edward became King, Rivers began the journey back to London with the 12-year-old boy, as ordered by the Council. On 29 April, the party was intercepted at Stony Stratford by the King's paternal uncle, Richard, Duke of Gloucester. After a convivial evening of eating and drinking with Gloucester and Buckingham, the following day Rivers was arrested, despite his nephew's protests, and sent to one of Gloucester's castles, where he was executed.

**Woodville, Catherine, Duchess of Buckingham and Duchess of Bedford, c. 1458 – 18 May 1497** The youngest sister of Queen

Elizabeth Woodville, she was married to the Queen's ward, Henry, 2<sup>nd</sup> Duke of Buckingham, by whom she had four children. The marriage is alleged to have been unhappy. When Henry VII became King, the widowed Catherine was married to his uncle, Jasper Tudor, Duke of Bedford. She married a third time to a far less exalted gentleman, presumably for love.

**Woodville, Sir Edward d. 1488** One of the younger sons of Sir Richard Woodville and Jacquetta, Duchess of Bedford, when his sister married Edward IV, he became a friend and companion of the King. He served under Richard, Duke of Gloucester in the Scottish wars, being knighted by Gloucester. On the death of Edward IV, Woodville was given the position of Admiral of the Fleet. When Gloucester became Richard III, the majority of the fleet accepted him, but Woodville, presumably aware of the execution of his brother, escaped to Brittany, where he joined Henry Tudor.

**Woodville, Elizabeth, Queen of England, 3 February 1437 – 8 June 1492** The oldest daughter of Sir Richard Woodville and Jacquetta, Duchess of Bedford, Elizabeth was married in 1453 to Sir John Grey of Groby, by whom she had two sons. She was widowed when her husband was killed at the second Battle of St Albans. In May 1464, Edward IV secretly married Elizabeth. When he was obliged to announce the marriage to his courtiers, many of whom were weighing up the relative merits of marriages to princesses of France, Italian duchies and Castile, the court was horrified. Elizabeth's low social position (derived from her father rather than her aristocratic mother) simply made her unsuitable to be a Queen. Edward's motives have usually been characterised as entirely based on personal affection, however Jones theorises that it was, at least in part, a deliberate decision to create a circle of supporters who would be entirely dependent on the King himself for favour and whom he could rely.

Elizabeth bore the King nine children of whom eight lived beyond infancy. It appears however that the Nevilles, at least, where never reconciled to her position. Some of the resentment can be attributed to the fact that her numerous brothers and sisters were married off to all of the wealthiest and most eligible heirs in the country. When Edward IV was forced into exile in 1470, Elizabeth retreated to sanctuary at Westminster Abbey where she gave birth to the couple's first son.

When Edward IV died, Elizabeth was not named as Regent for her son Edward V but a number of the nobles feared that she and her family would have too much influence over the boy, who was only 12. They agreed that it would be appropriate for Edward IV's brother, Richard, Duke of Gloucester, to become Lord Protector. When Elizabeth discovered that Gloucester had taken custody of Edward V and that her brother and her son, Sir Richard Grey, had been arrested, she took her younger son and her daughters back into sanctuary at Westminster Abbey. After prolonged persuasion she agreed to let her second son leave sanctuary to join his brother. The public were informed that Elizabeth's marriage to Edward IV had not been valid and that her son was not the legitimate King. Eventually, Elizabeth left sanctuary with her daughters who were received at the court of Richard III and his wife, Anne Neville. Elizabeth had entered into secret discussions with Lady Margaret Beaufort, Countess of Richmond, regarding the possibility that her eldest daughter, Elizabeth of York, might marry Lady Margaret's son, Henry Tudor, should he overthrow Richard III. When Henry Tudor did become king, Elizabeth was restored to her position as Queen Dowager and for the first years of Henry's reign was a central figure at court. She retired to a convent in 1490, whether willingly or under duress is disputed.

**Woodville, Joan, Lady Grey, d. before 1492**  Sister of Queen Elizabeth Woodville and sometimes named as Eleanor.

**Woodville, Sir John, c. 1445 – 1469**  Brother of Queen Elizabeth Woodville, he made a marriage so mercenary as even to shock the avarice of the time when he married Lady Katherine Neville, Dowager Duchess of Norfolk who was 45 years his senior. John Woodville was one of the men accused by Warwick of leading Edward IV astray and providing an excuse for his rebellion. Following the Battle of Edgecote, won by Warwick, Woodville was hunted down and executed.

**Woodville, Lionel, Bishop of Salisbury, c. 1447 – 1484** A younger brother of Elizabeth Woodville, who was Bishop of Salisbury from 1482. On Edward IV's death he went into sanctuary with his sister at Westminster Abbey and was attainted in the Parliament of January 1484.

 **Woodville, Richard, 1st Earl Rivers, c 1405 – 12 August 1469** Woodville was a retainer of John of Lancaster, Duke of Bedford and fought with him in France. On the Duke's death he secretly married the widowed Duchess, Jacquetta of Luxembourg, a presumption for which the pair were fined. He subsequently held a number of military positions under Henry VI. He fought for Lancaster at Towton but was reconciled to York thereafter. When Warwick rebelled and captured Edward IV, Rivers was one of the men that Warwick had hunted down to be given a show trial at Kenilworth Castle, following which he was executed.

 **Wyndham, Sir John, d. 1502** Associated with Edmund de la Pole, 3rd Duke of Suffolk, Wyndham was executed in 1502.

# Y

**Young, Thomas, MP for Bristol**. A loyal to Richard, Duke of York in the 1451 Parliament, Young suggested that the Henry VI should name an heir, suggesting York. This suggestion was greeted by an almost immediate                        dissolution                        of                        Parliament.

## Battles of the Wars of the Roses

| Date | Battle | Victor |
| --- | --- | --- |
| 22 May 1455 | 1st St Albans | York |
| 23 September 1459 | Blore Heath | York |
| 12 October 1459 | Ludford Bridge | Lancaster |
| 10 July 1460 | Northampton | York |
| 30 December 1460 | Wakefield | Lancaster |
| 2 February 1461 | Mortimer's Cross | York |
| 17 February 1461 | 2nd St Albans | Lancaster |
| 28 March 1461 | Ferrybridge | York |
| 29 March 1461 | Towton | York |
| 25 April 1464 | Hedgeley Moor | York |
| 15 May 1464 | Hexham | York |
| 26 July 1469 | Edgecote | Lancaster |
| 12 March 1470 | Losecote Field | York |
| 14 April 1471 | Barnet | York |
| 4 May 1471 | Tewkesbury | York |
| 22 August 1485 | Bosworth | Tudor |
| 16 June 1487 | Stoke | Tudor |

We'd love to know if you enjoyed this book. Please do leave a review.

www.ingramcontent.com/pod-product-compliance
Lightning Source LLC
Chambersburg PA
CBHW020508030426
42337CB00011B/280